GUIDE TO Electro-Motive E and F Units

JEFF WILSON

This book is dedicated to the memory of J. David Ingles. I met Dave in 1991 when I began working at Kalmbach, and over the years Dave became a friend as well as a colleague. He was an invaluable source of information about railroading, especially diesel locomotives, and was always happy to share his knowledge. Dave provided many photos for me for this project, and I wish he could have seen the finished product. Thank you, my friend.

Acknowledgements
In particular, I owe a debt of gratitude to three photographers who captured images of E and F units in color in the 1950s and 1960s. Thanks goes to Bob Milner, who began taking color photos in the early 1950s and whose travels enabled him to photograph trains throughout the country. Craig Willett took the time to search his slide collection, providing me with many outstanding images he captured of 1960s action. And thanks to the late J. David Ingles, whose work has long been featured in *Trains* and *Classic Trains,* and whose collection of images is unsurpassed. And I am indebted to all the photographers whose work resides in the David P. Morgan Memorial Library at Kalmbach Media. Without their work and contributions this book would not have been possible.

— Jeff Wilson, November 2021

Kalmbach Media
21027 Crossroads Circle
Waukesha, Wisconsin 53186
www.KalmbachHobbyStore.com

Published in 2022
26 25 24 23 22 1 2 3 4 5

Manufactured in China

ISBN: 978-1-62700-882-2
EISBN: 978-1-62700-883-9

Editor: Eric White
Book Design: Lisa Bergman

Library of Congress Control Number: 2021948188

On the cover: Boston & Maine FT A-B set no. 4221A/B and another F unit prepare to depart Mechanicville, N.Y., on freight MB-6 for Boston on an evening in the mid-1950s. The FTs dieselized the B&M's mainline freight trains when they arrived in 1943 and 1944, but they would soon be traded in on Geeps. *Jim Shaughnessy*

Back cover: A worker touches up the paint on the nose of a Chicago & North Western E unit in the 1940s. Railroads took pride in the complex schemes and logos on their E units, as they reflected the image they projected to the public of their passenger service. *Chicago & North Western*

CONTENTS

Amtrak is five years away as four Chicago, Burlington & Quincy E units, led by E9 9985A, lead a passenger train in June 1966.
Craig Willett

Allure of the E and F unit

Beginning in the late 1930s, Electro-Motive's streamlined E and F unit locomotives ushered in the diesel era with waves of color, capturing the public's attention while leading new passenger trains and—soon thereafter—heavy freight trains.

The public relations departments of EMD and railroads alike provided plenty of fodder for newspaper, magazine, and newsreel coverage of the new locomotives and trains, which for a public trying to recover from the Depression was met with excitement over the new technology.

The first E units followed the success of the integral diesel power cars of the early streamlined passenger trains of the mid-1930s, proving that diesels could be successful in fast passenger service. The first F unit—the FT—then proved that diesels could handle heavy freight service as well. And in both cases, not just that they could provide the service—but that they could do it more efficiently, more reliably, and more economically than any steam locomotive.

World War II interrupted diesel locomotive development. By the end of the war, many of the steam locomotives that had been overworked through the war's high traffic demands were old and simply worn out. Railroads needed new locomotives, and they wanted diesels—by the late 1940s, railroads were buying diesels as fast as manufacturers could build them. Although five manufacturers were building diesels at the time (Electro-Motive, Alco, Baldwin, Fairbanks-Morse, and Lima), EMD was by far the largest builder, and it was EMD's E and F units that largely replaced steam on mainline freight and passenger trains.
In 1934, when the first Electro-Motive Corp. diesel streamliner debuted

An F7A/F9B/F3B combo leads Northern Pacific's train no. 1, the *Mainstreeter*, at St. Paul, Minn., in 1967. The railroad was one of several that preferred F units over E units for passenger trains. The two-tone green scheme, which debuted in 1954, was designed by Raymond Loewy.
J. David Ingles

(Burlington's *Zephyr*), American railroads maintained 50,000 steam locomotives to carry trains to the tune of 17.8 billion passenger-miles and 268 billion freight ton-miles. By 1961, when the last mainline steam was gone, railroads needed just 28,500 diesels to carry even more traffic: 20 billion passenger-miles and 565 billion freight ton-miles.

In no way does the appeal of E and F units diminish the appeal or grandeur of steam. Steam locomotives are fantastic, wonderful, powerful, enthralling machines. The simple bottom line for railroads was that diesels proved early on that they were, hands-down, more reliable and more economical to operate—and not by a close margin. That's it. For railroads, it wasn't about aesthetics or history: it was about economics. Diesel locomotives were more expensive to purchase, but required less maintenance, far fewer people and facilities to maintain them, and fewer of them to do the same amount of work. The same basic locomotive model could be applied to a number of operations (fast freight, drag freight, passenger, heavy grades, flatlands, etc.) without the specialization of specific steam locomotive types.

Two E7s lead Chicago, Burlington & Quincy train 22, the *Morning Zephyr*, past the tower at Savanna, Ill., in October 1957. Many of the Q's late E units had stainless-steel side panels, including the lead E7 on this train.
Bob Milner

This book is a celebration of the early streamlined diesels from EMD. They provided a big splash of color in what had been largely a drab era of black locomotives and dark green passenger trains. Although some photographers were more focused on tracking down remaining steam locomotives than shooting diesels, we're lucky that many of them captured images of early Es and Fs in action. We're also fortunate that EMD did a good job of documenting its products with builder's photos, and the PR departments of railroads were also eager to capture their new acquisitions, especially in conjunction with new trains. In the following pages we'll look at the first diesel locomotives, how they led to the development of E and F units, and how Es and Fs evolved and improved over their 20-plus year production span. They were revolutionary diesels that provide a fascinating, colorful history.

ROSTERS AND INFORMATION

Throughout this book you'll find basic roster information by locomotive model, including number of locomotives owned by railroad and dates built. Numbering is not included for all models, as it was extremely complex for many railroads (many railroads renumbered their E and F units several times). The specific information comes from a number of sources. Electro-Motive's own data books were the primary source, then published rosters (especially those from the locomotive newsmagazine *Extra 2200 South)* and other periodicals and books—see the bibliography on page 192. These often don't agree, and you'll find published lists of production locomotives sometimes differ in number. This is often because of some locomotives being counted as new locomotives or as being rebuilt. If in doubt, check detailed rosters for the railroad in which you're interested.

CHAPTER 1

EARLY ELECTRO-MOTIVE DIESEL DEVELOPMENT

PREDECESSORS OF THE E AND F

Union Pacific's *City of Denver* M10006, built in 1936, was one of many early streamliners powered by Winton 201A diesel engines from Electro-Motive. The train, shown shortly after delivery, is led by two power cars designed to match the train, each with a 16-cylinder, 1,200-hp engine. The trend by the time it was built was moving away from power cars articulated to the train; these are separate units. *Union Pacific*

The eventual success of Electro-Motive's E and F units would not have happened without the company's pioneering work in developing gas-electric motor cars, diesel switching locomotives, and power cars for early streamlined passenger trains.

The complete dieselization of mainline passenger and freight trains by Es and Fs in the 1940s and 1950s began in the 1910s with increasingly powerful internal-combustion engines. It continued in the 1920s with continued development of diesel engines and the popularity of lightweight, self-propelled passenger cars that were more efficient than the steam locomotives they replaced.

Electro-Motive motor cars

The genesis of Electro-Motive traces back to 1912, when the Winton Engine Co. was formed as a subsidiary of the Winton Motor Carriage Co., a Cleveland-based company that began building automobiles in 1896. Winton Engine built large engines, namely

Electro-Motive started business in the 1920s building gas-electric motor cars ("doodle-bugs") like Chicago, Burlington & Quincy no. 9735. The company contracted with car builders for assembly—this one was built at Pullman in March 1929 with a 275-hp Winton gas engine. It was later refitted with a 400-hp diesel engine. *J. David Ingles collection*

diesel and distillate engines for stationary plants and marine use, as well as large gasoline engines for trucks.

The automobile industry in that period was evolving and growing rapidly, with a few large companies growing substantially while most small manufacturers were eventually pushed out of business. In Winton's case, its engine division proved successful, while the original motor carriage company struggled and eventually folded.

Electro-Motive itself started in 1922 as the Electro-Motive Engineering Corp., founded by Harold Hamilton and Paul Turner. It was soon renamed the Electro-Motive Co., or EMC. The company's goal was to build gasoline-electric railcars, often called doodlebugs or motor cars.

Motor cars had already found their niche in providing passenger service and less-than-carload (LCL) freight and express service on lightly traveled branch lines and secondary main lines. They were essentially self-propelled passenger cars, with a small gasoline engine providing enough power to pull itself and perhaps a trailing coach.

Motor cars were far more economical for these light-density lines compared to the cost of maintaining and operating a steam locomotive and one or two passenger cars (an EMC motor car could get about 4 miles to the gallon). Operating expenses in the late 1920s were reported to be about 50 cents per mile for a motor car, compared to $1.25 per mile for a steam train.

McKean had built the first motor cars in 1905, with General Electric also building its own line. They proved popular with railroads, but both builders' models suffered from control, mechanical, and operational issues. Electro-Motive saw a potential

Lehigh Valley no. 76 (formerly no. 116) is a boxcab switcher built by EMC in 1930 with a 400-hp gasoline engine. It's at Jersey City, N.J., in February 1949. *John F. Endler, Jr.*

General Motors used a pair of eight-cylinder Winton 201A diesel engines, each turning a generator, to power its display at the Century of Progress exhibition at the Chicago World's Fair from 1932-1934. *Electro-Motive Corp.*

market and sought to solve these issues with its own designs.

Electro-Motive's business model was unique, as the company didn't have its own factory or assembly plant. Instead it contracted with car builder St. Louis Car Co. (and later with Pullman and other builders) to manufacture the bodies and perform assembly, with engines supplied by Winton and electrical components from General Electric. The basic technology was simple: a small gasoline engine powered a generator, which provided electricity to traction motors on the car's leading truck.

The technology itself was sound, the basic system having been used for many decades for electric streetcars and interurbans. The key modification was bringing the power plant onboard in the form of a gas engine (instead of a stationary power plant and overhead electric wire), then figuring out how to best control the car's speed by regulating the speed of the engine.

Electro-Motive's motor cars were distinctive and proved to be popular. The first three were delivered in 1924 (to Chicago Great Western, Northern Pacific,

Santa Fe M.190, an EMC motor car built in 1932, introduced the idea of articulation, with the power car and baggage car sharing a truck. It was built by Pullman, powered by a Winton 12-cylinder, 900-hp distillate engine, had four powered axles, and could pull several trailing cars. *Trains magazine collection*

Union Pacific's M10000 was the first streamliner to hit the rails, in February 1934. The three-unit articulated train was built by Pullman and powered by a 600-hp Winton 191A distillate engine, as the 201A diesel wasn't yet ready for service. The train embarked on a 16,000-mile publicity tour after it was built. *Trains magazine collection*

CANADIAN NATIONAL 9000 AND 9001

The first road passenger diesel in North America was Canadian National's two-unit no. 9000, built by Canadian Locomotive Co. in 1928. Each was powered by a 1,330-hp, V-12 Beardmore diesel engine. *Canadian National*

Several years before Electro-Motive began providing prime movers for articulated passenger train motor cars, Canadian National became the first North American railroad to operate high-speed trains powered by separate diesel-electric locomotives. Boxcab diesel-electric locomotives 9000 and 9001 (originally both were numbered 9000) were built by Canadian Locomotive Co. (CLC) in November 1928 and April 1929. Each was powered by a 1,330-hp V-12 diesel engine furnished by Beardmore, a Glasgow-based company that produced engines, aircraft, and locomotives; electrical gear was from Canadian Westinghouse. Baldwin provided designs for the bodies, which were assembled at CLC in Kingston, Ontario. They were designed to carry passenger trains at 70 mph.

Their design followed contemporary heavy-electric locomotives, with a boxcab body and a cab at the lead end only. Each had large driving wheels (51" diameter) on four powered axles and smaller non-powered wheels on leading (four-wheel) and trailing (two-wheel) trucks. In diesel and electric terms, this gave them a wheel arrangement of 2-D-1 (2=unpowered two-axle truck; D=four-axle powered truck; 1=one-axle unpowered truck). The wheel arrangement matched a contemporary 4-8-2 steam locomotive.

The two became the first diesel passenger locomotives to lead trains in North America, pulling the second section of CN train 15, the *International Limited*, from Montreal to Toronto on August 26, 1929. Through the next decade the locomotives served both together (they were the first locomotives operating with multiple-unit controls) and separately on various passenger trains. When working, they performed well; however, reliability was lower and maintenance time and costs higher than hoped for, and no further locomotives were built.

Both were removed from service and stored in 1939. The 9000 was rebuilt in 1943, its Beardmore engine replaced by a 16-cylinder EMD 567A engine. It was given armor plating to serve as a guard train at Prince Rupert, B.C., during World War II. In 1945 the plating was removed and 9000 continued in passenger service until being retired and scrapped in 1946.

The first diesel-powered streamliner, in April 1934, was Chicago, Burlington & Quincy's *Zephyr* (later renamed *Pioneer Zephyr*), no. 9900. The three-unit train, built by Budd, featured fluted stainless-steel construction and was powered by an eight-cylinder 600-hp Winton 201A diesel.
Louis A. Marre collection

and National of Mexico). Business grew quickly: in 1925 the company sold 18 railcars, and EMC would eventually sell more than 400 doodlebugs. Power ranged from early 175-hp engines to later 400- to 600-hp versions, and cars were built in many lengths and configurations.

A key moment for Electro-Motive came in 1928 when a General Electric engineer who had been working with EMC on its motor cars left GE to join EMC as its chief engineer. Richard M. (Dick) Dilworth would prove to have a great understanding of designing locomotives by blending all the required components, and he would be the driving force in directing several locomotive projects over the next three decades.

Enter General Motors

By the late 1920s, General Motors had emerged as a major corporation in the U.S. Its share in the automobile market was growing, and the company was looking to expand its business in heavy applications for diesel engines and other related products. Instead of starting from scratch, GM in 1930 got a jump in the market by first acquiring Winton (in June) and then Electro-Motive—which had suffered a severe drop in sales with the coming of the Depression—making them subsidiaries. Initially, EMC was made a subsidiary of Winton, with EMC's task becoming marketing Winton's engines for railroad use. The companies would eventually emerge as the Winton Engine Corp. and Electro-Motive Corp.

General Motors' purchase of EMC and Winton triggered the developments that would eventually sweep steam from mainline railroading with the FT. General Motors provided solid corporate backing, guaranteeing that Winton would have financial stability as well as personnel and other resources for development—something that small, independent manufacturers and suppliers simply didn't have, especially in a depression.

A railroad that's considering investing in a multi-million dollar (that's 1930s dollars, mind you) locomotive order is much more likely to do so with a solid company like GM, rather than a small company that could possibly be out of business before (or shortly after) the order is completed.

The GM backing allowed Winton and EMC engineers and designers to look at engine and locomotive design from a railroad outsider's point of view, purely for what internal-combustion could do well on railroads. The companies were not tied to current locomotive manufacturers' (or railroads') traditional views of steam power, nor would they look at diesels as being limited in potential.

The 16-cylinder Winton 201A engine is cleaned and polished just after installation in Union Pacific's M10004 *City of San Francisco* power unit. *Electro-Motive Corp.*

Why the diesel?

Winton, now with GM's Charles F. Kettering directing engine design (and Charles' son Gene as an engineer), now had the resources to begin developing diesel engines that could be smaller, yet more powerful, than the then-current typical stationary power plants, making them useful for portable, moving platforms (such as trains, submarines, and ships).

Winton and EMC were not alone in applying internal-combustion to railroad locomotives. In fact, the American Locomotive Co. was first, having partnered with GE and Ingersoll-Rand to build several small boxcab diesel-electric switchers starting in 1925, and Canadian Locomotive Co. built two road locomotives in 1928 (see "Canadian National 9000 and 9001" on page 12). Electro-Motive itself built a trio of 400-hp boxcab switchers in 1930 and 1931, with bodies built by Bethlehem Steel, using Winton Model 148 gasoline engines. Two went to Lehigh Valley and the third to a steel mill.

In that era, the biggest challenge in building a diesel-electric locomotive was the diesel engine itself. Diesels had been around since the 1890s, and had proven to be quite successful for many applications. They had evolved considerably, but they were for the most part large, cumbersome, and slow. They worked best as stationary units (as in a power plant) where they had plenty of space, received constant attention, and were free of external forces (such as the shocks of bumping along rails or being subjected to sub-zero winter or desert summer temperature extremes).

Reliability was extremely important. As a power plant or on a ship, an engine could receive constant attention and care. This was not the case on a locomotive, where engines would travel long periods of time unattended, with no maintenance other than refueling and occasional checking of oil and water levels.

So, with all of these challenges, why were EMC and others pushing for diesel and not gasoline engines? Size and power

The *Flying Yankee* of Boston & Maine and Maine Central was quite similar to Burlington's *Zephyr.* Also built by Budd, no. 6000 had a 600-hp Winton 201A power plant. *Electro-Motive Corp.*

Electro-Motive opened its McCook, Ill. (LaGrange) factory in 1936, enabling the company to finally perform assembly of its locomotives. On May 10, 1936, the assembly floor held Union Pacific's *City of San Francisco's* power units and several diesel switchers. *Electro-Motive Corp.*

were limiting factors. Gasoline engines were reaching their largest practical limits with the 300- to 400-hp engines used by gas-electrics. Diesels were more efficient, had more power potential, and were longer lasting. Gasoline was also much more expensive than diesel fuel.

What gave diesels the advantage was that they didn't require a spark to ignite fuel in the cylinder, as was necessary in a gas engine. Instead, the high temperature that resulted from the piston compressing air in the cylinder ignited the fuel. This eliminated the need for spark plugs and the resulting electrical system. It also meant diesel engines had to be built heavier and stronger, but this also meant they were more durable and long-lasting, with stronger components that didn't wear as quickly.

For mobile applications, one intermediate solution was the distillate engine. These could be larger, more powerful, and more efficient than gasoline engines. As their name implied, these ran on "distillate"—which included a range of less-refined fuel from kerosene to naptha or light oil, which were less expensive than gasoline. These engines, however, still required a spark to ignite, and doing this was more difficult than gasoline. Since distillate wasn't as volatile, the engines required multiple spark plugs in each cylinder. Coupled with the heavier fuel's tendency to foul the plugs quickly, this meant distillate engines required more maintenance and had lower reliability and availability.

The ultimate solution to building successful internal-combustion locomotives would be developing a diesel engine that was compact, reliable, and powerful.

The Winton 201A diesel engine

The breakthrough for EMC came in 1932 with the development of the Winton Model

Burlington no. 9906A and B (*Silver King/Silver Queen*) were built for the *Denver Zephyr* in October 1936. They retained *Zephyr* stainless steel and shovel-nose design, but were built as separate locomotives on their own four-wheel trucks. The A unit has a pair of 12-cylinder, 900-hp 201A engines; the B has a single 16-cylinder, 1,200-hp 201A. *Electro-Motive Corp.*

Illinois Central's *Green Diamond* poses for a publicity photo on April 2, 1936. It was the last fully articulated streamliner. Built by Pullman (and resembling Union Pacific's streamliners in style), it was powered by a 16-cylinder, 1,200-hp Winton 201A diesel engine. *General Electric*

201 diesel engine, a V-style design that produced 600 hp (with the eight-cylinder version). It was initially designed for naval submarines, but adaptable in various sizes (number of cylinders) to a locomotive frame.

One important feature of the 201 design involved using a welded block with separate power assemblies and components (instead of a larger cast-iron block). The major innovation was a compact fuel injector that measured and delivered fuel into the cylinder. The injectors eliminated the long fuel input lines that had been needed on earlier diesels. The result was a smaller, lighter engine than earlier designs.

Each cylinder of the 201 had an 8" bore and 10" stroke, with a 502 cubic-inch displacement per cylinder. It was a two-cycle (or two-stroke) design, compared to other contemporary diesels, which were four-cycle engines. In a two-cycle engine, only two strokes of a piston (one downward, one upward—one revolution of the crankshaft) accomplish all tasks: admitting air and fuel, compressing the fuel/gas, ejecting exhaust gas, burning fuel pushing the piston down, and ejecting exhaust gas; as opposed to a four-cycle, which takes four

Electro-Motive demonstrator boxcabs 511 and 512 paved the way for the E units to come. The bodies were built by GE; each was powered by two 12-cylinder, 900-hp Winton 201A engines. *Electro-Motive Corp.*

strokes (two up, two down, one of which is a power stroke; two revolutions of the crankshaft).

A two-cycle engine requires fast action on the part of cylinder ports that admit and expel fuel, combustion air, and exhaust gas. It is a simpler design and is more powerful for a given size; a downside is fuel efficiency—which, with the cheap fuel of the era, was not as big a consideration as it would be for the modern era.

The 201 would be produced in 6-, 8-, 12-, and 16-cylinder versions. Early versions were problematic, namely with fluid leakage and cylinder heads. Revisions resulted in an upgraded design, the 201A, which is what eventually entered production.

General Motors had a large exhibit at the Chicago World's Fair in 1933-1934, and installed a pair of 201A engines in a public display area to power GM's Century of Progress exhibit. The engines were still being tested as they were installed, and still had issues to be worked out, according to EMC's Gene Kettering. Engineers managed to get them working reasonably well, and they drew the attention of many—including some railroad officials.

Baltimore & Ohio EMC boxcab no. 50 entered service in 1935, carrying the *Royal Blue* between Washington and Jersey City. *A.P. Formanek*

First streamliners

While engine development was progressing, EMC and GM were still working with railroads and car builders to develop power plants for trains. A harbinger of the streamlined, articulated trains that would soon appear was an extension of the gas-electric doodlebugs that EMC had already been building. The Santa Fe was looking for a larger, more-powerful version that could pull multiple trailing cars at higher speeds. The resulting design, built in 1932, was Santa Fe motor-baggage car M.190. It was the first articulated train, with the front end of the 60-foot trailing baggage car supported by the rear power truck of the 22-foot motor car. Unlike conventional doodlebugs, which had one powered truck, the M.190 had a pair of two-axle power trucks.

The power plant was the largest internal-combustion railroad engine used to that point: a 12-cylinder, 900-hp version of Winton's Model 194 distillate engine. This was a big, heavy engine, with 9 x 12 cylinders (9" bore, 12" stroke).

During 1933, the Chicago, Burlington & Quincy and Union Pacific were both working on new lightweight, articulated

Santa Fe's EMC box-cabs (nos. 1 and 1A, the "One-Spot Twins") initially had a protruding housing over the air-intake grilles on the ends, along with *Super Chief* lettering.
Trains magazine collection

Santa Fe rebuilt its boxcabs, elevating the cab and giving the end a pug-nosed appearance. It also swapped the original four-wheel trucks for six-wheel versions. *Trains magazine collection*

trains to be pulled by internal-combustion engines supplied by EMC. Both wanted the trains to be displayed at the Century of Progress exhibition.

The first one delivered, in February 1934, was Union Pacific's M10000 streamliner, which featured a three-unit articulated train with a combined power car/baggage/Railway Post Office and two smooth-sided passenger cars. Built by Pullman, it featured a smooth, streamlined aluminum shell painted yellow and brown, led by a high-perched cab over a bulbous nose with prominent grille.

The engine supplied by EMC was a 600-hp Winton 191A distillate engine. The UP had wanted a diesel to power it, but opted for the distillate engine to get the train in service faster as the Winton 201A was not quite ready for service. Upon delivery, it began rolling across the country on a 16,000-mile exhibition and publicity tour.

The UP's engine choice made the second streamliner in service the first powered by a diesel: CB&Q's *Zephyr*, an articulated, three-unit streamlined train built by Budd, featuring fluted stainless-steel sheathing. The power car featured what became known as a shovel nose, with operator's cab right at the front of a slightly sloped front end, with air-intake grilles above the cab.

The shovel-nose power car received, at Burlington president Ralph Budd's (no relation to the train builder) insistence, an improved 201A Winton diesel. It began its own cross-country tour upon its delivery in April 1934. The *Zephyr* gained fame by making a non-stop (13-hour, 4-minute) dawn-to-dusk run from Denver to Chicago to kick off the second year of the Century of Progress fair on May 26, 1934. Both trains remained on display in Chicago for several months. The *Zephyr* entered revenue service in November, running between Kansas City and Lincoln; the UP train began service between Kansas City and Salina, Kan., in January 1935.

The UP and Burlington trains garnered a lot of publicity from both the trade press as well as newspapers and magazines. Both were extremely popular on their tours, drawing millions of visitors. Both showed that the diesel was capable of pulling trains and doing it fast.

More streamliners follow

Several other new trains and power cars followed, most of which used versions of the Winton 201A. The *Flying Yankee,* built by Budd for the Boston & Maine and Maine

Central, entered service in April 1935. It was visually quite similar to the *Zephyr,* with a shovel-nose cab on the power car of a three-unit articulated set.

Burlington (Budd) and UP (Pullman) both ordered additional train sets for progressively longer trains with more amenities, which required larger power plants. The UP's M10001, the *City of Portland,* was completed in 1934 and entered service in May 1935 as a seven-car train powered by a 1,200-hp Winton diesel. It was the first streamliner with sleeping cars for its Chicago-Portland run; it was followed by four additional streamliners (serving San Francisco, Los Angeles, and Denver from Chicago) built through August 1936.

Burlington ordered a pair of articulated trains (the *Twin Zephyrs*) to serve its Chicago to Minneapolis/St. Paul corridor, followed by a pair of longer *Twin Zephyrs* when ridership on the first *Twins* exceeded their capacities, then another three trains. The total included four power cars with 8-cylinder engines (9900-9903), built through October 1935, followed by four with pairs of 12-cylinder engines (1,800 total hp; nos. 9904, 9905, 9906A, 9907A), plus two B units with single 16-cylinder, 1,200-hp engines (9906B, 9907B) through October 1936, then a final stand-alone shovel-nose locomotive, no. 9908, in 1939, with a 12-cylinder, 1,000-hp engine.

The Illinois Central's *Green Diamond,* delivered in May 1936, was the last fully articulated train/power unit built. The five-car train was built by Pullman and powered by a 16-cylinder 201A rated at 1,200 hp.

Two other power cars worth mentioning are Seaboard Air Line nos. 2027 and

Baltimore & Ohio rebuilt its boxcab with a shovel nose in April of 1936 and repainted and relettered it for service on the *Abraham Lincoln* on its Alton subsidiary. *Baltimore & Ohio*

Seaboard Air Line power car 2027 (and sister 2028) was another transition toward separate locomotives for trains. Built in April 1936 with *Zephyr*-like styling, it's powered by an 8-cylinder Winton 201A and could pull several cars. *Seaboard Air Line*

2028. These were shovel-nosed motor cars built by St. Louis Car Co. in 1936 with eight-cylinder Winton 201A engines, each with a single powered truck. They housed baggage/Railway Post Office sections, and they could pull additional cars.

These early passenger trains and power cars showed that diesel power was not limited to slow speeds and switching locomotives. The focus, however, was definitely on the train as a whole, not the individual power car. On late deliveries for both UP and CB&Q, the power units were built as separate locomotives; however, they retained the styling of the trains they served, and they were intended to power those specific trains.

Until the mid-1930s, EMC still did not have its own assembly plant. The doodlebugs were still built and assembled at various car builders; the power plants for articulated trains were installed at the builders of the train sets.

Seeing potential for growth and increased business, in 1935 EMC broke ground on a new factory in McCook, Ill.—it would become known as the LaGrange plant, as McCook didn't have its own mailing address. The new factory would serve as a locomotive assembly plant, with the engines themselves still built by Winton in Cleveland. It opened in 1936, with the first locomotive emerging in May, making EMC a full-blown locomotive manufacturer.

Boxcab passenger locomotives

The idea of a diesel passenger locomotive as a separate interchangeable unit was still not widely accepted. Railroads, however, were realizing some limitations with articulated trains. They had advantages: The articulation saved weight, making a lighter train, and improved operation by eliminating slack action and providing a smoother ride. However, if anything goes wrong with any part of the train—power car, engine, passenger car truck—the entire train must be taken out of service for repair. Articulated trains are also inflexible: in high-demand seasons additional cars can't easily be added, and even if they can, the train is limited by what its power unit can pull.

With several streamlined power units under its belt and a new factory being built, EMC built a pair of test/demonstrator locomotives in August 1935, followed by three production models, to gauge their feasibility. The idea wasn't new—remember

FIRST DIESEL-ELECTRIC LOCOMOTIVES

Electro-Motive wasn't the first company to produce diesel-electric locomotives. The American Locomotive Co. (Alco), previously a steam builder only, teamed up with General Electric (which had built many successful heavy electric locomotives) and Ingersoll-Rand (which produced engines) to build more than 30 300- and 600-hp diesel-electric boxcab switchers in the 1920s. A 300-hp Alco-GE-IR locomotive in 1925 is credited as the first. Alco was a pioneer in end-cab switchers, with its HH ("high hood") 600-hp locomotive debuting in 1932, using the MacIntosh & Seymour 531 diesel engine.

Alco was the most forward-thinking and progressive of the steam locomotive builders when it came to diesels, and the company became Electro-Motive's primary competitor in the diesel market through the E and F unit era. Although steam builders Baldwin and Lima eventually both dabbled in the diesel market, they both remained focused on steam too late. Neither devoted enough resources to diesel design and development; both fell behind in the market and were out of the locomotive business in the 1950s.

Credit for building the first diesel-electric locomotive goes to the Alco/GE/Ingersoll-Rand conglomerate, which built several small boxcab switchers starting in 1925. Baltimore & Ohio no. 1 was powered by a 300-hp, six-cylinder inline four-stroke diesel. *General Electric*

the 1920s Canadian locomotives (see page 12)—but would incorporate all that the company had learned from its earlier projects.

Because its factory wasn't yet ready, EMC contracted to have the bodies built by General Electric, and they (not surprisingly) had the basic styling of boxcab electric locomotives. Providing the power for each was a pair of 900-hp, 12-cylinder Winton 201A diesel engines. Each engine/generator supplied power to traction motors on one truck; electrical gear was from GE.

The locomotives rode on four-wheel trucks of a design that eventually became known as the AAR type B road truck; all axles were powered. This truck was an equalized, swing-bolster design that used

Electro-Motive built six TA passenger diesels for Rock Island for its *Rocket* trains in August 1937. The four-axle, single-engine (16-cylinder Winton 201A), 1,200-hp locomotives followed basic E unit styling. *Rock Island*

both coil and leaf springs. It was a relatively simple design, and versions of it would be built into the 1970s.

A key part of the design was that each boxcab could be operated as a separate locomotive, or they could be joined together electrically and operated by one engineer as a single locomotive, taking advantage of the principle of multiple-unit (MU) building-block operation. Both were double-ended, with cabs on each end, reflecting a common design of heavy electric locomotives.

The two demonstrators were numbered 511 and 512, and would test on several railroads. Production models in late 1935 included a pair for Santa Fe (nos. 1 and 1A) and a single locomotive for the Baltimore & Ohio (no. 50). The demonstrators would be scrapped in 1938, but the others would have reasonably long service lives.

The first to enter revenue service was B&O no. 50 in August 1935, carrying the *Royal Blue* (Jersey City to Washington, D.C.). Less than a year later, the locomotive was reassigned to B&O subsidiary Alton to carry the *Abraham Lincoln* (Chicago to St. Louis). Its nose was rebuilt with a shallow taper (giving it a shovel-nose-like look) in April 1936 prior to beginning that service.

The Alton officially acquired the locomotive in 1943 when it became independent; it went with the railroad into Gulf, Mobile & Ohio when it merged the Alton in 1945. As GM&O no. 1200, the locomotive had its shovel nose removed, returning it to near- original appearance, and it remained in local freight and commuter service until it was retired in 1956. It's now preserved at the National Museum of Transport in St. Louis.

Santa Fe's pair entered service in September 1935 to cover the *Chief* (and had the train's lettering and logo on the front). They had a unique appearance, with an over-arching radiator housing over the front cab windows. Their paint scheme was initially green, scarlet, and blue.

The AT&SF modified its locomotives several times, first with the addition of a second headlight, with some windows modified and some covered. In 1938 the front ends were modified, giving them a tall, pug-nosed appearance (sometimes called a "semi-turret" cab), and a three-axle truck was added to the front (these were added to the rear as well in 1940). They would both be rebuilt later.

The locomotives performed well in service, but their status was largely as experimental or test units. Electro-Motive took several lessons forward as it developed the future E unit line. The boxcab bodies

The Burlington staged this publicity photo in 1944 upon delivery of its first FT, no. 100, coinciding with the 10th anniversary of the *Zephyr*, which had recently passed 1.6 million miles of service. Note the diminutive stature of the streamliner. *Chicago, Burlington & Quincy*

proved to be crowded: having two engines/generators in one locomotive took up a lot of interior space, pushed the weight limits for a four-axle locomotive, and didn't provide adequate space for fuel and steam-generator water. The four-wheel trucks didn't provide the smoothest or most-stable ride, especially at high speeds. And the flush-end-cab design, although fine for switching or slow-speed freight work, was not popular among engine crews running at high speeds.

Another significant locomotive appeared at the same time EMC began production of E units in 1937: six four-axle TA locomotives for Rock Island in 1937. This still reflected the era of custom orders, where locomotives were separate items but still built for a railroad and/or train, and were not off-the-shelf models. The six TAs (nos. 601-606) were stand-alone locomotives, and had design elements that foreshadowed the F units that would follow two years later.

The passenger units, designed for the railroad's *Rocket* streamliners, had a long, sloped nose like the E1/EA, but rode on a pair of four-wheel trucks and were each powered by a single 1,200-hp Winton 201A (as opposed to the twin engines of the six-axle E units). No provision was made for being able to run them in MU fashion with other locomotives.

Transition

Along with the passenger boxcabs and power cars for streamliners, EMC had begun turning out its first end-cab switchers in 1936 with the SC and SW, both of which used the Winton 201A diesel. All of these helped the company's development of E units and, eventually, F units.

The first of what became the E unit line of locomotives were built for Santa Fe and Baltimore & Ohio in 1937. Although the first Es were still largely custom locomotives, they paved the way for the standardized models that would soon follow.

To make this happen, engine and locomotive designs continued to evolve. The 201A engine had been revolutionary and enabled much of this progress, but even after continued revisions and modifications, it still had several problems. It became obvious that the ultimate solution was an all-new engine design. (Gene Kettering later offered what became a famous summary of the 201A: "I don't recall any problems with the dipstick.")

Winton in 1937 became the Cleveland Diesel Engine Division of GM, and the company would soon develop a new diesel engine—the 567—that would be a vital feature of the new locomotives. The era of the E and F unit was about to begin.

CHAPTER 2

DAWN OF THE E UNIT

SLANT-NOSE DIESELS LED TO STANDARDIZED MODELS

Baltimore & Ohio EA no. 56 rests at St. Louis between runs just after World War II. The EAs debuted Electro-Motive's E unit line, and are marked by their inset headlights and small number boards compared to later Es. Note the three-dimensional B&O emblem on the nose. *Henry J. McCord*

56
B&O
GULF

By the late 1930s, the use of diesel locomotives in passenger and switching service was no longer a novelty. Railroads were moving on from building new streamlined, lightweight passenger trains as articulated sets, and were shifting from integral power cars to separate locomotives. The diesel business was also growing, moving away from steam for many applications.

Although now separate units, locomotives were still being built as custom power cars assigned to—and designed to match—specific trains. This would start to change as Electro-Motive began building the first of its streamlined, six-axle stand-alone E unit passenger locomotives: the EA for Baltimore & Ohio, E1 for Santa Fe, and E2 for Union Pacific. The locomotives were built concurrently; the EAs and E1s were delivered from April 1937 to June 1938 and the E2s from October to December 1937.

E unit design

Although the appearance of the new locomotives gave a nod to some of the earlier power cars, the sleek, streamlined E units were a radical departure from EMC's earlier boxcabs and from any other stand-alone switching locomotive.

In designing the new locomotive, EMC took what it learned from the four-axle, twin-engine boxcabs built for B&O and AT&SF, along with the lessons from the multiple power units that led trains of Burlington, UP, Illinois Central, and others. A big advantage in 1937 was that EMC was finally able to design and build full locomotives, including the bodies, at its new plant in LaGrange, Ill., instead of relying on passenger-car builders and other contractors to do the assembly (and in most cases to lead the design).

For the E, the company stuck with the twin-engine design of the earlier boxcabs, as they allowed a powerful single-unit locomotive. A major design change, however, was to place the body atop two six-wheel trucks, a change from the four-wheel trucks of earlier power cars and locomotives.

EMD had found the boxcabs, although decent performers, to be heavy, with the space inside the body very crowded with equipment. Stretching the body length provided more room, and six-wheel trucks allowed better weight distribution. In each truck, the two outboard axles were powered

Baltimore & Ohio EA no. 51 and a matching B unit lead the westbound *National Limited* at Crusher Curve west of Hopewell, Va. The B&O's EAs were similar to Santa Fe's E1s, but had rounded side windows. *W.R. Osborne*

by traction motors; at the center was an unpowered "idler" axle, used to help spread weight and provide a smoother ride. This gave E units a designation of A1A-A1A.

The new trucks were noticeably different from any earlier designs, and they turned out to be a great decision. They had a distinctive appearance and were informally named the "Blomberg" truck after their designer, Martin Blomberg (Blomberg would eventually be awarded more than 100 patents). Blomberg had joined EMC in 1935 from Pullman, where he had been heavily involved in both truck and carbody design. Although the name is unofficial, it's a designation that became almost universally used.

The long (14'-1") wheelbase, three-axle Blomberg truck earned a reputation as a smooth-riding, low-maintenance truck that is also easy on track. In technical terms, it is flexible compared to most earlier four-wheel designs. It has outside spring hangers between wheels, giving it very good lateral stability, and it lacked drop equalizers. Coil springs above the journal boxes isolate the

Santa Fe E1 no. 2 poses just after delivery in 1937. It was initially assigned to the *Super Chief*. The E1 has taller side windows than the EA, and the window ends are squared instead of rounded.
Santa Fe

truck frame from wheel shocks, improving the ride and reducing component wear, and all axles are equipped with roller bearings.

A clever design was making the bolster hollow and making it serve as a duct for the traction-motor cooling air. This eliminated the need for separate blower ductwork.

The trucks use 36"-diameter wheels, compared to the 40" wheels of later freight units. The 36" wheels are lighter than 40" wheels, saving overall weight; the lower profile also gave the locomotives a lower center of gravity, providing smoother high-speed operation (especially on curves). With a few minor refinements over the years, the A1A Blomberg remained the standard truck through the end of E unit production in the 1960s.

The "E" in E unit designations initially stood for "eighteen hundred horsepower," the initial total rating from the two 12-cylinder Winton 201A diesels that powered each locomotive. Each powered a generator, each of which provided power to the two traction motors on one truck. The engines were oriented so that the generator ends were at the rear of the locomotive, with a power takeoff at that end to turn the radiator fans. Most of these early Es used General Electric electrical equipment, with Westinghouse gear on a few locomotives.

The Es feature cabs placed above and behind long noses. This provided better visibility and a higher degree of safety compared to boxcab or shovel-nose designs, some of which had the operator at the very front of the cab—an undesirable position in a high-speed locomotive. Some early power cars had cramped, small cabs, with engine components that protruded into the cab. The E units had roomier cabs, with a wall between the cab and engine compartment.

Engineer's controls on the E established the basic standard for all following Electro-Motive passenger and freight cab units. From the engineer's seat on the right side, the throttle stand was on the left, with an eight-notch controller handle and the

A Baltimore & Ohio EA body takes shape on the floor at the new Electro-Motive plant in 1937. *Electro-Motive Corp.*

BLOMBERG A1A TRUCK

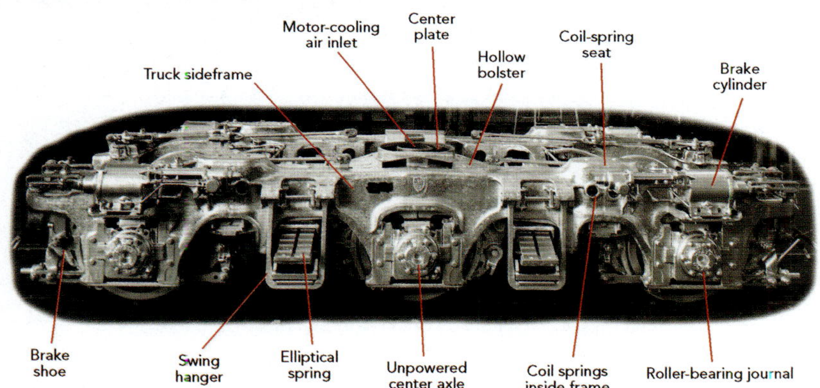

The six-wheel A1A truck designed by Martin Blomberg was used under all E units. It was a revolutionary design praised for its smooth-riding, stable characteristics. *Electro-Motive Division*

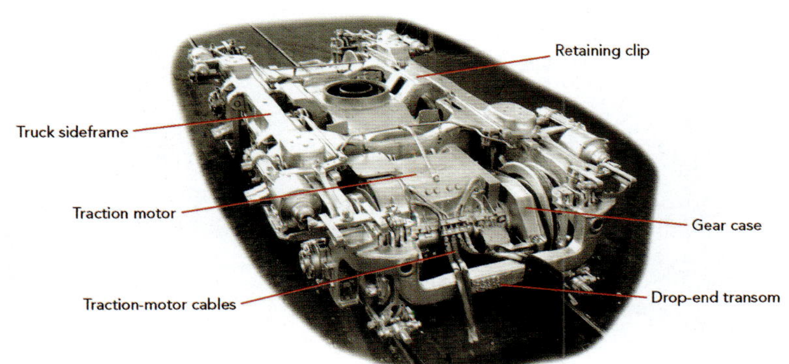

The early E units established the basic cab control setup that would be used on all succeeding E and F units. The throttle stand is to the left, brake stand to the right. *Electro-Motive Division*

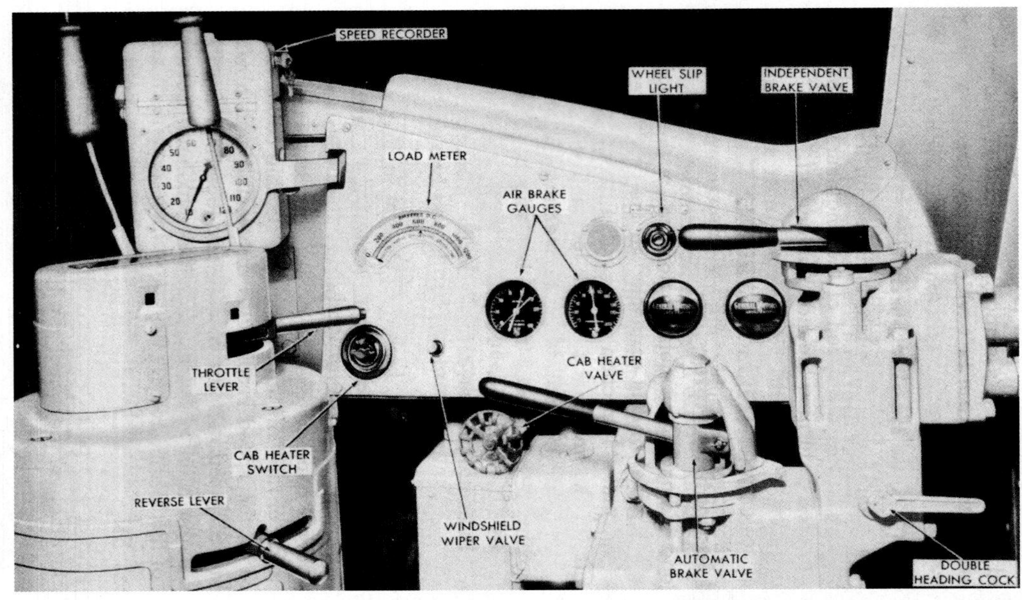

Santa Fe E1 no. 2 poses for a publicity photo with the streamlined *Super Chief* shortly after delivery. Numbers 2 and 2A were initially assigned to the train when delivered. *Santa Fe*

EARLY E UNIT PRODUCTION

EA, EB	A units	B units	Numbers (B units in parentheses)	Dates built
B&O	5	6	51, 53-56 (51B-56B)	5/37-6/38
E1				
ATSF	8	3	2-9 (2A-4A)	6/37-4/38
E2				
UP *	2	4	SF-1, LA-1 (SF-2, -3; LA-2, -3)	10-12/37
E3				
ACL •	2	0	500, 501	11/39
ATSF	1	1	11 (11A)	8-9/39
C&NW	4	0	5001A, 5001B, 5002A, 5002B	5-6/39
CRI&P	2	0	625, 626	7/39
FEC	2	0	1001, 1002	11/39
KCS **	3	0	1-3	4/39-6/40
MP	2	0	7000, 7001	10/39
UP	1	0	LA-5	3/39
E4				
SAL	14	0	3000-3013	10/38-11/39
E5				
CB&Q	11	5	9909A-9915A, 9950A, 9980A (9910B-9912B), 9914B-9915B (9950B, 9980B)	2/40-6/41
E6				
ACL	22	5	502-523 (750-754)	11/40-4/42
ATSF	4	3	12-15 (12A, 13A, 15A)	4/40-5/41
B&O	8	7	52, 57-63 (57x-63x)	9/40-7/41
C&NW	4	0	5005A, B; 5006A, B	8/41
CRI&P	5	0	627-631	6/40-11/41
FEC	3	1	1003-1005 (1051)	12/40-2/42
IC	5	0	4000-4004	10/40-12/41
KCS	2	0	4, 5	1/42
L&N	16	0	450A-457A, 450B-457B	5-9/42
MILW	2	0	15A, 15B	9/41
MP	2	2	7002, 7003	10/41
SAL ***	3	0	3014-3016	11/39-12/41
SOU	7	4	2800-2802, 2900-2903 (2900B-2903B)	3-5/41
UP *	8	4	7M1A, 7M2A, 8M1A, 8M2A, 9M1A, 9M2A, LA-4, SF-4 (LA-5, -6; SF-5, -6)	8/40-3/41

* E2 ownership was divided among UP, C&NW, and SP.
• ACL 501 was in a wreck before delivery and rebuilt by EMC to E6 specifications.
** KCS no. 1 was former EMC demonstrator 822.
*** SAL no. 3014 was former EMC demonstrator 1940.
This roster reflects early E units as built, with original road numbers.

Above: The E2 had a large, bulbous nose in a similar style to UP's earlier M-series streamliners. Internally the E2 matched the EA and E1. Only two A-B-B sets were built—no. SF-1, assigned to the *City of San Francisco,* was owned jointly by Union Pacific, Chicago & North Western, and Southern Pacific.
Electro-Motive Corp.

Above right: The E2 A-B SF-1 and SF-2 were covering the *City of Denver* in April 1941; they're shown here paused at 40th Street in Denver.
Richard H. Kindig

reversing lever below it. The transition lever was on the left of the throttle stand.

The brake stand was directly ahead and to the right, with the automatic (train line) brake valve handle in front and the handle for the independent (engine) brake above it and to the right. Gauges on the control panel showed air brake reservoir and train line pressure, with the ammeter/load meter at left and the speedometer and speed recorder at upper left. Engineers praised E units for their excellent view from the cab, their safety, and their smooth riding characteristics.

The long (about 70 feet for the EA-E2) bodies were about 7 feet longer than EMC's boxcabs (which also lost interior space to cabs at each end), allowing more interior room for the engines and control equipment. The length also made it easier to locate the fuel tank under the frame between the trucks.

A key in the design of the body was that the sides weren't simply walls riding atop the frame. Instead, the sides were built as a truss (modified Howe design) structure that provided structural strength tied to the frame. The side surfaces were panels of metal-sheathed plywood, held at their joints by batten strips over the side trusses. This construction technique allowed a lighter underframe with significant strength, and was used on all subsequent E and F diesels. Locomotives built this way became known as carbody diesels or cab units.

The E unit bodies abandoned the use of front grilles for radiator air intake (which had been especially prominent on power

An eclectic mix of motive power is on hand at the Omaha engine servicing facility during World War II, including, from left, early Chicago & North Western E units; a pair of Union Pacific's M-series streamliners; Chicago & North Western E3 no. 5001B; and SF-1, the *City of San Francisco* E2 (at far right), sporting a war-era headlight shroud.
Trains magazine collection

STEAM GENERATORS

By the 1930s, passenger cars relied on steam not just for heat, but air conditioning as well. Steam was supplied by a steam line running back from the locomotive through all cars, connected at each joint by threaded pipe connections. With steam locomotives, trains had a ready supply; however, when diesels were leading, a separate steam source was needed.

The solution was the steam generator, a diesel-fuel powered device that heats water to steam and feeds it to the steam line. Although sometimes referred to simply as "boilers," steam generators are more complex than that. Outside manufacturers supplied the devices to the diesel builders, with Vapor-Clarkson and Elesco the major builders.

A steam generator works by pumping water through a series of coiled pipes inside a combustion chamber. The coils are heated by a flame provided by diesel fuel, fed by an atomizer, much like a fuel-oil furnace (or an oil-fired steam locomotive). Steam generators come in various configurations, and are listed by their rated capacities in pounds of water evaporated per hour, with typical sizes ranging from 1,700 to 4,500 pounds. The sizes chosen by railroads vary by locomotive type, estimated usage, train length, and the number of locomotives typically assigned to a train. Long trains and trains operating in severe winter climates require much more steam capacity than short trains in warm climates.

Steam generators were operated by the fireman, with a control panel in the fireman's side of the locomotive cab that included controls as well as gauges indicating water tank level and steam-line pressure. These remote controls had varying levels of reliability, and firemen still sometimes found themselves going back through the locomotive (or locomotives) to tend to the steam generator, especially on early models.

The steam line connections were not as simple to connect or separate as the air hoses of the brake and signal lines, which is one reason why switching passenger equipment was more time consuming than switching freight cars. You can see the steam pipe connections at the ends and pilots of passenger locomotives; photos taken in winter often have telltale wisps and clouds of steam water vapor at loose connections and valves.

By the 1970s, many new passenger cars relied on electricity for heat, A/C, and accessories. This was supplied by the locomotive, usually by a small diesel engine powering an alternator. Called HEP (head-end-power) units, they eventually replaced steam generators in many E and F units that remained late in passenger service, especially those serving commuter lines.

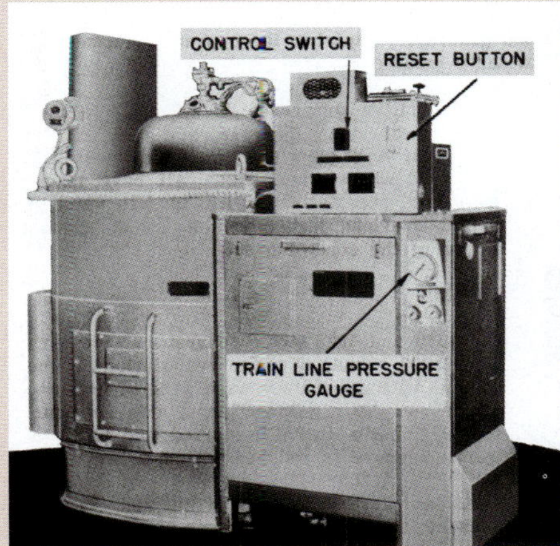

This Vapor-Clarkson model 4630 steam generator has a capacity of 3,000 pounds per hour. It was a common model used in E units. *Electro-Motive Division*

Steam escapes from the steam-line pipe on the pilot of a passenger-service F unit. *Trains magazine collection*

Electro-Motive E3 demonstrator no. 822 tests on the Alton in 1938, leading train 19, the *Ann Rutledge,* at Springfield, Ill. The recessed headlight would not appear on production E3s. *J. David Ingles collection*

cars of Burlington, UP, and IC trains). Air intakes were relocated to the upper sides (openings covered by screen), with air drawn in by fans located above the radiator cores and under louvered openings in the roof. This provided even air flow for cooling regardless of direction of travel, which had been an issue with front grilles.

A steam generator was located at the rear of the locomotive, with a vent and exhaust stack on the roof directly above it (see "Steam Generators" on page 35). Water-supply tanks for the steam generator were located under the cab floor of A units and in the carbody itself on B units (in the space where the cab would be).

Production models

The honor of the first E units to emerge from EMC goes to Baltimore & Ohio nos. 51 and 51A, an A-B set of EAs that rolled out of the factory on April 19, 1937. They

Santa Fe bought just one E3A (and a matching B), no. 11, built in August 1939. Note the rooftop louvers are now flush with the roof. *Electro-Motive Corp.*

Chicago & North Western E3 no. 5002 was built in June 1939. The slats in the rooftop grilles are perpendicular to the roof and protrude slightly. The C&NW did not use the nose number boards, painting them over. The protruding headlight housing became standard on the E3. *Chicago & North Western*

were formally dedicated at Washington Union Station on April 25, then made their first run to Chicago on the point of the westbound *Capitol Limited.* The B&O bought 12 EAs (6 A units, 6 Bs).

All three railroads receiving the EA, E1, and E2 had already been EMC passenger-diesel customers: Santa Fe and B&O for EMC's pioneering boxcab passenger units and UP for the power units for its streamlined, articulated passenger trains.

The Santa Fe put its E1s (8 A units, 3 Bs) in service on the *Super Chief,* then the *El Capitan* and other trains. The UP had two A-B-B sets of E2s—one assigned to the *City of San Francisco* streamliner and the other to the *City of Los Angeles*.

Although virtually identical internally, the EA, E1, and E2 all differed in external appearance—the era of true off-the-shelf models wouldn't come until the E3 and later models. The EA and E1 are very

Round portholes were a custom element on Union Pacific's lone E3A. It was delivered as SF-5 in March 1939 (with B unit SF-6), renumbered 5-M-1A in 1941, then 951A in 1946. It's shown here being serviced in September 1949. It was later renumbered again, to 991, and traded in on an E9 order in 1956.
John P. McGlynn

similar. Both have the same nose shape, with inset headlights instead of separate protruding housings (as on later Es) and tiny illuminated number boards on each side of the headlight.

Both have grille-covered rectangular air intake openings at the top of each side, with windows in the panels below them. However, the windows differ in style: The EA windows aren't as tall, their pattern varies (two- or three-panel), and their left and right ends are rounded. On the E1, the windows are taller, in a different pattern (two three-panel and one single-panel), and have squared corners.

The two E2 A units have unique rounded ("bulbous") noses with protruding headlights and round side portholes in a 3-3-1 pattern instead of rectangular windows. The overall styling of the E2s was based on the railroad's earlier articulated power units, but otherwise the E2s mechanically were identical to the EA and E1.

These locomotives could carry their trains at better than 100 mph. The trucks could have several gear combinations, which varied starting tractive effort and maximum speed. Most E units used a gear ratio of 52:25 (the number of teeth on the large gear on the axle and the small pinion gear on the traction motor), which allowed a maximum speed of 117 mph; other available gear ratios included 55:22 (100 mph), 56:21 (92 mph), and 57:20 (85 mph).

Railroads operating fast trains in flatlands preferred the high-speed gear ratios, while those running trains at lower speeds or in hilly and mountainous regions opted for low-speed gear ratios, which provided more tractive effort at starting and allowed a lower minimum continuous speed. The E unit was designed and built for speed, and was at its best when pulling passenger trains long distances over fairly level terrain.

Although there were cases where railroads ran Es on trains through

Florida East Coast bought two E3As, nos. 1001 and 1002, in November 1939. Here no. 1001, the *Henry M. Flagler,* makes a station stop in the 1940s. Note the water-fill hatch below the cab window and the sand-fill hatch below the number board. *B.F. Cutler*

mountainous territory and on heavy grades, the use of helpers was often needed. The Santa Fe, among other railroads, reassigned its Es to level routes while opting for other locomotives (including F units) in mountain territory because it was unhappy with how the E units performed on tough grades.

Recognizing that the locomotives would be used on trains of varying lengths, with railroads using one, two, or more units, EMC provided the option of cabless B units—something originally used on some of the earlier Burlington and UP power cars. Operationally, a B unit was the same as an A unit for a given model. There were three initial reasons railroads opted for B units: B units were slightly less expensive, lacking the cab and control equipment of an A unit; importantly to some railroads, the B blended with the leading A unit, allowing an unbroken viewing line from the lead locomotive through the passenger cars, with all having matching paint and lettering schemes; and—especially important in the early days of diesels—an A-B or A-B-B set was considered a single locomotive, and couldn't be challenged by an operating union as being two locomotives (and thus requiring two separate operating crews—a contested point into the early 1940s in some areas until railroads reached agreements with the Brotherhoods).

Aesthetics and the relatively small cost savings eventually gave way to operational considerations, as railroads found it easier logistically to have a cab on every locomotive. Most later E models were built with nose-mounted multiple-unit (MU) connections; many early Es had the connections added during their service lives. This was especially true by the mid-1950s as passenger train miles were dwindling and railroads were far more concerned with the bottom line than with the aesthetics of having perfectly matched locomotives on a train.

Kansas City Southern no. 1 is former EMC demonstrator no. 822. The original recessed headlight has been replaced with a now-standard housing; the upper intakes have a grille covering instead of the usual screen.
Louis A. Marre collection

The early Es continued the color explosion initiated by the various articulated trains of the mid-1930s. Santa Fe's E1s notably introduced that railroad's red and silver "warbonnet" scheme, a swooping design by GM artist Leland Knickerbocker that would become a trademark for the railroad. Many of the early locomotive and train paint schemes were developed by GM artists: study them, and although the colors vary among railroads, you'll see that the designs have a definite family resemblance in how they use stripes, patterns, and curved color-separation lines to accentuate the shape of the locomotive nose.

These early Es served well through the 1940s, but their temperamental Winton engines and early electrical gear was not as reliable as the 567-engined E units to come. Almost all were rebuilt in the 1950s to E8 specifications (as E8Am and E8Bm), with the others retired and scrapped.

These locomotives were an important step toward standardization, but they still

Missouri Pacific's two E3s, 7001—shown at St. Louis in April 1946—and 7000, were built in October 1939. They were customized with portholes and curved side trim. They were also unusual in that they did not use EMC electrical gear: no. 7001's is from Westinghouse; 7000's is from GE.
Louis A. Marre collection

The E4 was a customized E3 built only for Seaboard Air Line, with the addition of a nose door and nose multiple-unit (MU) connections (small hatch to the left of the headlight). Number 3001 sports *Orange Blossom Special* lettering in its October 1938 builder's photo.
Electro-Motive Corp.

followed the idea that a model number was assigned to a specific railroad order. As EMC kept fine-tuning the designs, the number of variations would drop as the company's sales increased; next to come was a standard locomotive that could be ordered by any customer.

The E3 and the revolutionary 567 engine

The Winton 201A engine, as significant a factor as it was to expanding EMC's railroad business and launching its passenger-locomotive line, remained trouble-prone. A number of fixes and modifications had been performed and attempted, but even as the first Es were being built, it became apparent that a better solution was needed. In 1936, engineers went to the drawing board to design an all-new locomotive engine, using what they'd learned from the 201A.

The result in 1938 was the Model 567 engine, named for the 567-cubic-inch displacement of each cylinder—larger than the 201A, with an 8½" bore and 10" stroke (compared to 8 x 10 and 502 cubic inches). The new engine would, with periodic upgrades and revisions, serve in all of Electro-Motive's cab diesels (and other locomotives) through the 1950s.

Like its predecessor, the 567 is a two-cycle, V-style design, but with cylinder banks at a 45-degree angle compared to 60 degrees for the 201A (making the 201A narrower but taller). The 567 is non-turbocharged, instead using a Roots blower to force combustion air into the engine. The Roots blower pushes less air, resulting in less power than a turbocharger, but was cheaper, less complex, and far more reliable than contemporary turbochargers. The cylinder heads and other components were also completely redesigned.

The nose door on the E4 was a housing that pulled outward from the nose to a vertical position, then allowed the door to open inward. This view also shows the retractable (hydraulically controlled) coupler. *Electro-Motive Corp.*

Chicago, Burlington & Quincy E5 A-B 9912A/9912B (*Silver Meteor* and *Silver Comet*) were built in March 1940. Note the fluted sides and lettering panel between the windows and screened openings. The shrouds above the trucks were decorative and got in the way of maintenance; they were removed after a couple years of service. *Chicago, Burlington & Quincy*

Burlington local No. 27 from Kansas City has arrived in Omaha behind E5 9915B on a cold February day in 1962. The E5 was a custom E6 built for CB&Q, featuring stainless-steel sheathing and fluted side panels. *J. David Ingles*

The 567 was more powerful than the 201A, and more importantly proved to be more reliable and easier and more economical to maintain. It was built in several configurations; E units would use the 12-cylinder design, while later F units would use a 16-cylinder engine and some switchers the 6- and 8-cylinder models.

The new engine allowed EMC to upgrade its passenger diesel design. The resulting locomotive, the E3, was a groundbreaking effort. It was EMC's first passenger diesel that was designed as an off-the-shelf model that any railroad could purchase (although EMC still customized versions of it for two railroads as the E4 and E5). Even though only 18 E3s were built, eight different railroads purchased them. They were built during a very short period, April to November 1939, when improvements would result in an upgraded design, the E6.

Mechanically the E3 was noteworthy. It was the first locomotive to receive the new 567 engine, using two 12-cylinder versions, giving the locomotive 2,000 hp—a bump of 200 hp compared to Winton-engined Es. The generator position was swapped

Chicago & North Western E6 5005A poses for its builder's photo in August 1941. The E6 would kick off the era of diesel passenger locomotives used in general assignment pools instead of being assigned to individual trains.
Electro-Motive Division

ELECTRO-MOTIVE E3 AND E6

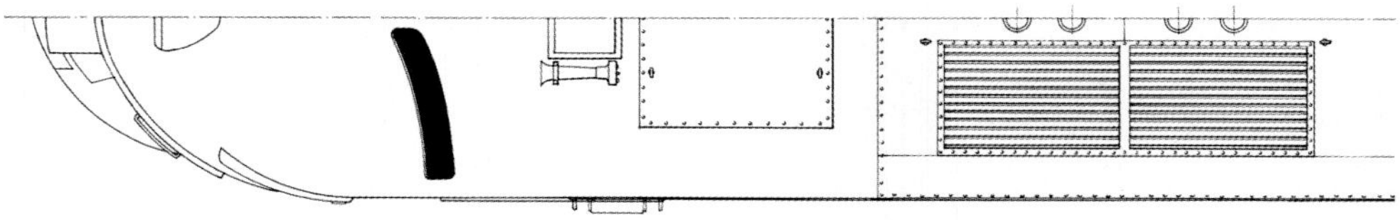

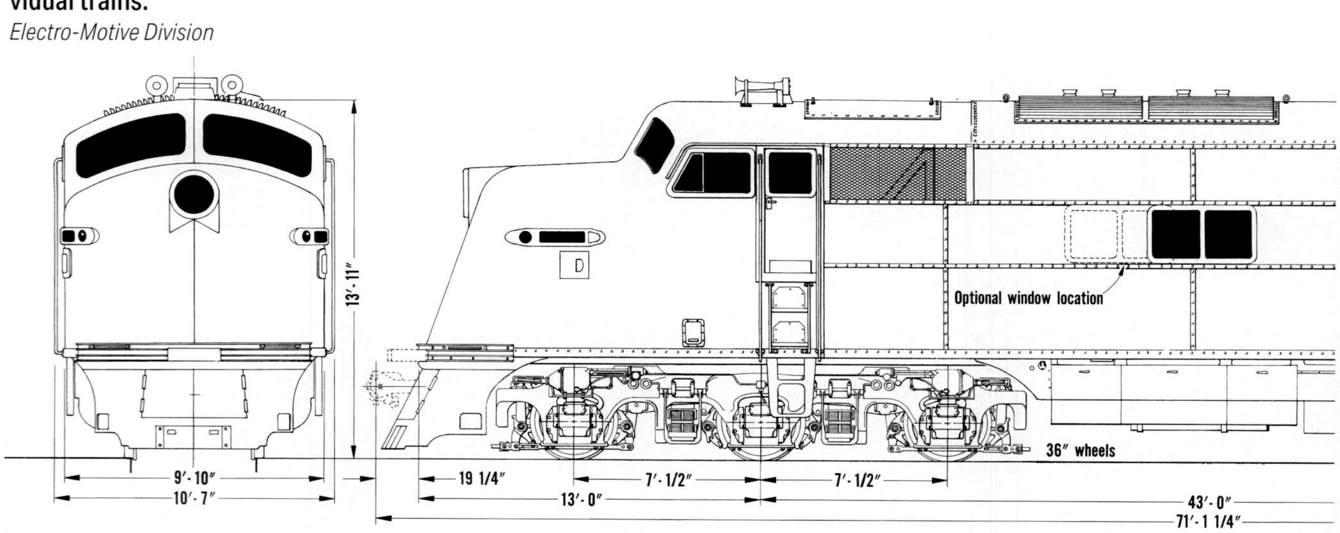

E6 VARIATIONS: THE AA AND AB6

Although the era of customized locomotives was drawing to a close by the time the E6 was in production, EMC built two notable variations of the E6 in August 1940.

The AA (or AA6) was a single locomotive built for Missouri Pacific, designed to lead the *Delta Eagle*, a two-car train operating between Memphis, Tenn., and Tallulah, La. Number 7100 (upper right) looked like a standard E6 A unit (albeit with portholes), but it had just a single 567 engine in the forward position and was rated at 1,000 hp. The rear of the locomotive interior served as the train's baggage-express compartment, with baggage doors on each side. The locomotive remained in service until its train was discontinued in 1962.

The AB6 (bottom right) was a response to Rock Island's operations of its *Rocky Mountain Rocket*. The train ran from Chicago westward to Limon, Colo., where it split into two sections—one section to Colorado Springs, the other to Denver. To handle the smaller Colorado Springs section, the railroad ordered a custom locomotive that was basically an E6B, but with operating controls and a cab in the squared-off end, and a single 567 engine (rated at 1,000 hp). With the full train coupled together, this locomotive—designated an AB6—was coupled behind a standard E6A, keeping the appearance of a standard A-B locomotive set until the train sections were separated. The Rock bought two of them, nos. 750 and 751.

Both AB6s eventually received a second 1,000-hp engine (in 1948 and 1949), but they retained their end cabs. They had long service lives after being bumped from streamliner service, carrying Chicago commuter trains into the 1970s.

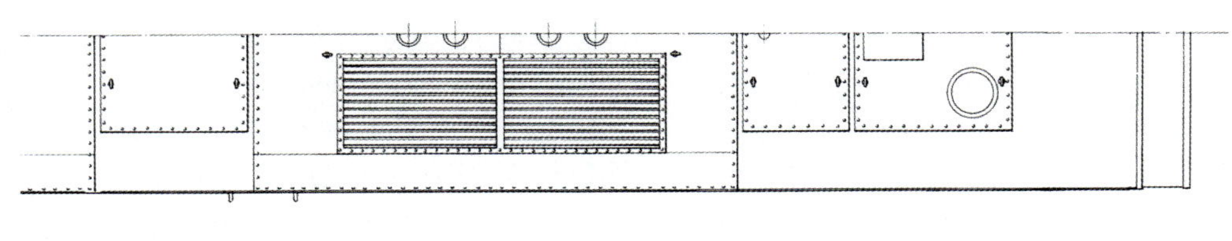

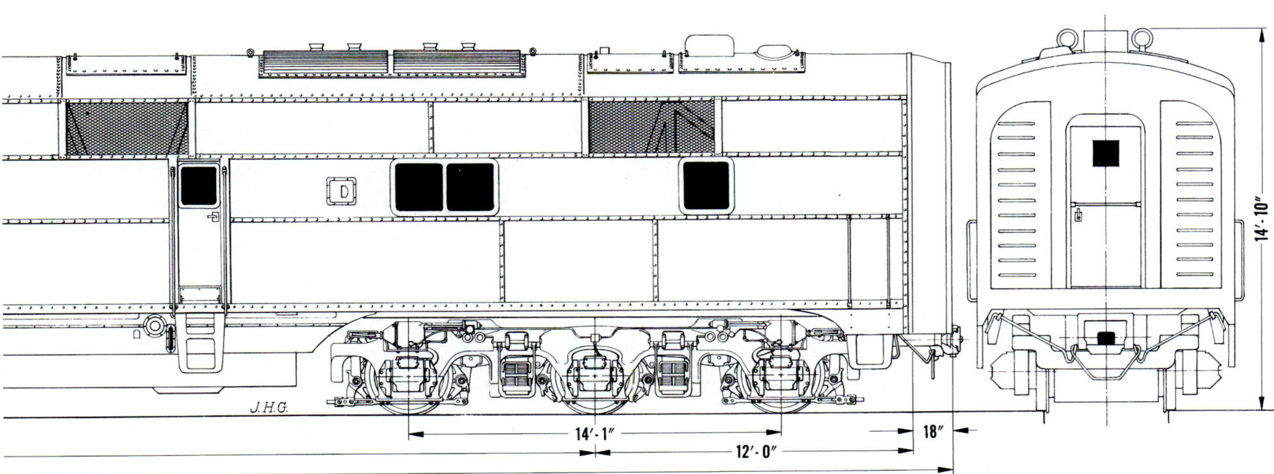

The basic dimensions of the E3 and E6 remained the same, but many details differed (even among individual orders), including rooftop louvers and batten-strip locations. *Kalmbach Media*

The Union Pacific acquired A-B-B E6s SF-4, -5, and -6 when it re-equipped the *City of San Francisco* with a new 14-car consist in early 1941. As with the E2s assigned to the earlier version of the train, the E6A carries the logos of all three host railroads on the nose. The cast pilot is unique to UP E units. *Union Pacific*

to be in front of each engine. The exhaust stacks were centered on the roof over each engine. The cooling system was completely redesigned, with a separate radiator housing above each cylinder bank, with louver-covered fans on either side of the stacks. Radiator fans were still mechanically powered, belt-driven by each engine.

With the E3, EMC began building its own generators and traction motors. It had relied on GE for electrical equipment for most earlier locomotives and power cars (the exceptions being Westinghouse supplying motors and generators for B&O's EAs and one A-B-B set of E2s). The move reflected EMC's growing locomotive business, having its own manufacturing plant, and wanting to have less reliance on outside suppliers of major components.

Electro-Motive built a demonstrator locomotive, no. 822, to show off the many improvements and upgrades. It left the factory in April 1938, leading trains on several railroads.

Externally, the E3 had the basic body style and slanted nose angle and contour of the EA/E1, but with a headlight that protruded from the nose in a housing, with the lens face vertical. This provided better forward light projection and together with small number boards and classification lamps at each side of the nose gave them a distinctly different look than earlier Es. (Demonstrator E3 no. 822 was built with the early headlight, but was rebuilt before entering revenue service.)

The carbody sides had rectangular openings with air-intakes covered by screens (upper) and windows (lower), and closely resembled the E1 design. Parts of the truss framing were visible through both the screened openings and windows.

Production models began appearing in March 1939 (but a custom variant for Seaboard Air Line, the E4, began appearing in October 1938). The demonstrator was purchased by Kansas City Southern and became its no. 1.

Cosmetic variations to the basic E3 included the two Missouri Pacific locomotives and the single Union Pacific example, all of which received round portholes on the side (two sets of double portholes on MP sides; triple portholes on the UP sides). Rock Island's two E3As had a downward taper at the rear of the roof, allowing the roof to slope down to match the level of the Rock's passenger-car roofs.

Milwaukee Road received its only prewar E units, E6 A-A set 15A/15B, in October 1941. *Milwaukee Road*

The E4 and E5 were special cases, where model designations were given to locomotives designed for specific railroads. In both cases, the locomotives were internally identical to their base models (E3 and E6) but with distinctive external features.

The E4 was a customized E3, built exclusively for Seaboard Air Line. The first seven were built from October 1938 to January 1939; the last seven in November and December of 1939. What made them unique was that they were the only early E units (through E6) equipped with nose doors, as SAL anticipated the need to operate the locomotives at times in "elephant style" (nose-to-tail). The design of the slanted nose made impossible what would become conventional nose access doors on F units and E7 and later E units. The solution was a pivoting door housing that pulled out from the nose to a vertical position, then opened to the inside (seen in the photos on pages 41 and 42). This would allow safer passage between locomotives in motion.

The E6s on Santa Fe's *Super Chief* are fueled and watered at Albuquerque, N.M., in March 1943. Numbers 15 (L) and 15A were built in May 1941, and the headlight cover is a World War II requirement for locomotives operating on the West Coast. Initiating diesel service required fuel stations at intermediate locations. *Jack Delano, Library of Congress*

Santa Fe E6 no. 13 is serviced in Dallas in August 1966. Body modifications include a distinctive lower twin-beam headlight and number in the forward side window. The railroad's E6s would be stored within two years. *J. David Ingles collection*

The E6

The next step in the standardized passenger locomotive line was the E6, with the first emerging in November 1939. Visually, the E3 and E6 were virtually identical. About the only spotting differences were changes in batten-strip locations and a change in the roof-top louvers or air intakes. Fans on early E units were under the roof, covered by slatted louvers (the E8 and E9 had fans in visible housings on the roof). On the E6, these louvers ran lengthwise above each engine location, with two sets of louvers straddling the engine exhaust stacks, which followed the roof center line. On most E3s, these louvers ran cross-wise in panels. This can be a difficult feature to spot, as most photos of these were taken from ground level looking upward.

Internally, the E3 and E6 were both powered by two 12-cylinder 567 engines, with EMD's own D4 generators and D7 traction motors; both were rated at 2,000 hp. The engine, however, was upgraded. The original 567 engine had a U-shaped cast-steel top deck in the crankcase; this

Baltimore & Ohio was third in E6 ownership with 15. Number 1409 in the final simplified blue scheme is paired with an E8B on a passenger train in October 1966. *Craig Willett*

Southern E6 no. 2900 and an E6B pose for a publicity photo with the *Tennessean* in 1941. The Southern owned 11 E6s: 7 A units and 4 B units.
Southern Railway

piece proved to be prone to cracking and was replaced by a fabricated welded deck. Although engine power and ratings remained the same, the engines were known as 567U and 567V to differentiate them. The lubricating oil system was also upgraded.

The E5 was a customized E6, built specifically for Chicago, Burlington & Quincy and its Colorado & Southern and Fort Worth & Denver subsidiaries, with the first delivered in February 1940. Burlington had been a customer for its *Zephyr* power cars, and had extensively tested EMC's boxcab demonstrators 511/512 (in fact, they were on the railroad long enough to be painted silver). The E3 demonstrator, no. 822, also spent extensive time on the CB&Q.

The Burlington was sold on the E unit, but still wanted customized locomotives to match its growing fleet of fluted stainless-steel passenger cars. The result was an E6 but with a stainless-steel body, including fluted stainless sides to match the railroads' Budd-built passenger cars. The E5 also

Louisville & Nashville was second in E6 ownership, buying 16—all A units—from May to September 1942. They were the last E units built before production ceased during World War II. Originally nos. 450-457A and B, in 1946 they were renumbered 750-757 and 770-777.
Electro-Motive Division

The Southern modified the side panels of E6 2901 with portholes as well as air-intake filters covered by louvers. Built in April 1941, no. 2901 and an E7 are on the *Tennesseean* at Lynchburg, Va., in July 1959.
J. David Ingles collection

had shorter side windows than standard E3s and E6s, allowing room for a lettering panel between the side windows and upper screened openings.

The success of the earlier E unit models was reflected in that all buyers of E1s through E4s returned to buy E6s. Electro-Motive had proven to be responsive in upgrading its offerings, acknowledging problems and correcting them, and providing good, reliable products that railroads could depend upon. A total of 133 E5s and E6s were built for 15 railroads until War Production Board restrictions stopped production in September 1942.

The E6 took advantage of the country's improving economy, with many railroads investing heavily in streamlined passenger equipment (and entire trains). Although some were sticking with steam, many railroads wanted new diesels to pull their new trains. Although the automobile was taking its share of travelers from trains—especially for branch, secondary, and short-haul routes—railroads were still the kings of long-route intercity travel. Along with railroads' heavy investment in new equipment, many launched extensive advertising and marketing campaigns to direct the traveling public to their new trains, and many of these ads featured the new diesels prominently.

The colorful new diesels caught the eye of the public. The large, smooth sides of E units were like empty painters' canvases waiting to be filled. The early E unit era saw

Illinois Central's five E6As enjoyed long service lives. Here E6 4003 and an E8 lead train 6, the *Panama Limited*, at Homewood, Ill., in June 1969. The 4003 was built in December 1941. It has been modified with new side portholes and air-intake louvers.
J. David Ingles

the dawn of dozens of colorful, ornate paint schemes and intricate patterns, lines, and lettering that complemented their railroads' passenger-car paint schemes.

The success and growth of EMC's diesel locomotive line, including switchers and its new road freight locomotive, the FT (introduced in 1939—see Chapter 3), led General Motors to create the Electro-Motive Division of GM, effective January 1, 1941. The new EMD assumed all locomotive production from EMC, along with all related product and railroad engine production from the Cleveland Diesel Engine Division (EMC ceased to exist; Cleveland continued in business building marine and stationary engines).

Wartime transition

The United States' entry into World War II in December 1941 changed the railroad industry, and in particular affected production of locomotives and rolling stock. Beginning in 1942, the War Production Board strictly controlled how critical materials could be used and what could be produced with them. Locomotive production was curtailed (see Chapter 3, page 72 for a more detailed description).

For EMD, which had became heavily involved in producing diesel engines for naval vessels, this meant the WPB no longer allowed EMD to build road passenger diesels, with the last E6s delivered in late 1942. However, unlike other diesel locomotive manufacturers, which were only allowed to build switching locomotives during the war, EMD was allowed to continue building its successful FT road freight diesels (with the WPB controlling the number produced and their allocation).

Electro-Motive took advantage of this, applying lessons learned from the FT and adding its knowledge from earlier E units to develop a new locomotive line that would debut at the end of the war. For passenger service, this would mean the introduction of the best-selling passenger locomotive ever, the E7, as Chapter 4 explains.

The long, sleek nose was a distinctive trademark of Electro-Motive's early E units. Illinois Central E6 no. 4001 is at speed with train 8, the *Creole,* near Tolono, Ill., on April 2, 1960.
J. Parker Lamb

CHAPTER 3

F MEANS FREIGHT

THE FT REVOLUTIONIZED RAILROADING

An A-B-B-A set of Santa Fe FTs eases a westbound freight downgrade at Tehachapi in California in 1949, putting its dynamic brakes to good use. The Santa Fe was the first railroad to order FTs and owned the most (320). Number 110 was built in May 1942. *Linn Westcott*

SANTA FE
110

By 1939, diesel-electric locomotives had proven themselves capable in switching and fast passenger service. Freight trains, however, remained the domain of steam. Electro-Motive's FT would change that, and in a course of just six years, the complete dieselization of U.S. railroads was inevitable.

Dignitaries are on hand as FT demonstrator 103 tests on Rio Grande at Denver on April 28, 1940. The EMD dynamometer car is tucked behind the locomotives, followed by crew and supply cars, then the train. *Richard H. Kindig*

The first four-unit FT—an A-B-B-A set of four 1,350-hp diesels totaling 5,400 hp—left EMC as a demonstrator locomotive in November 1939. The two A-B pairs making up the set were initially numbered 1030 and 1031, but this was changed to 103 for the full locomotive. In the next 11 months, no. 103 pulled trains on 20 railroads in 35 states, putting on 83,764 miles in showing it could handle all types of trains in all types of territory and in conditions ranging from triple-digit desert heat to sub-zero winter cold. (See the map on pages 56-57 to see where the FT traveled.)

Unlike many other rollouts of new trains and technology of the day, the FT's demonstration run was kicked off by virtually no promotion: there were no ceremonies with reporters from newspapers and magazines, or photographers, or men in suits; no ads in the trade press; no effusive predictions of how the locomotives would dominate railroading; and no construction photos. There was just quiet communication with a group of railroads that Electro-Motive thought would be interested in testing a new kind of freight power. Although there were publicity and photo opportunities at many points during the locomotive's travels, the initial goal for EMC wasn't a grand publicity tour; it was truly to test the new locomotives under real-world conditions to see if they would perform as planned.

The demonstrator locomotives no doubt turned many heads among trackside observers who might be used to seeing diesels on passenger runs, but not freight trains. The demonstrator paint scheme was relatively subdued compared to most passenger streamliners: dark green with buff yellow striping that curved around the nose, highlighting its shape. The lettering was

Number 103 tested on passenger trains as well as freight. Here the FT demonstrator stays on schedule pulling the 17 cars of Northern Pacific's ***North Coast Limited*** in the Jefferson River Canyon near Limespur, Mont., in March 1940.
W. R. McGee

not fancy, with GM initials on the nose and ELECTRO-MOTIVE spelled out on the A-unit sides. What called attention to them was that they weren't on passenger trains, but pulling freight trains—heavy freight trains—something not seen before.

The railroads, by and large, were willing to try out the FT but many were skeptical. The general consensus among most railroad operating officials of the day was that freight was best handled by steam. The new wave of modern Super-Power steam locomotives that were entering service were powerful, fast machines. Many were rated at 5,000 hp or more, and they featured improved efficiency and performance compared to earlier steam locomotives. Even railroads that were already successfully running diesels in fast passenger service were not sold on the idea of diesels for freight. Diesel-powered passenger trains were relatively light, but still required helpers in some areas. Long-term maintenance and durability were still an unknown. Railroads didn't have fueling stations or maintenance facilities for diesels, nor did they have workers familiar with the technology. And a big factor: a new diesel could cost about double that of a steam locomotive, with price per horsepower up to triple that of steam (a new A-B set of FTs in the early 1940s cost about $230,000).

Demonstrator 103 first left LaGrange in early November, making a test run on Baltimore & Ohio and returning to the plant. Then, after a final tune-up, the FT set headed west on the Burlington on November 25. In the next 10 months, no. 103 ran in all types of service, pulling fast freights on flatland railroads, lugging heavy freight trains on mountain grades, and even leading passenger trains. Railroads put the demonstrator to the test, running the engines hard in A-B pairs as well as the full four-unit set, pushing the limits of tonnage to see how the locomotives responded. The

FT 103 TOUR

Electro-Motive's demonstrator FT, four-unit set no. 103, headed west from LaGrange to begin its demonstration tour in November 1939. Over the next 11 months, the locomotive led trains on 20 railroads in a wide variety of operating conditions. At almost every step the FT outperformed the steam locomotives that were then doing the job. The map at right shows the routes the demonstrator traveled, with highlights from each railroad. That the tour was a rousing success is evidenced by the fact that 16 of the 20 railroads that tested the FT ordered production locomotives; the four that didn't buy FTs bought later-model F units. A total of 1,096 FTs was built until production ended in November 1945, establishing Electro-Motive as the premier builder of diesel locomotives.

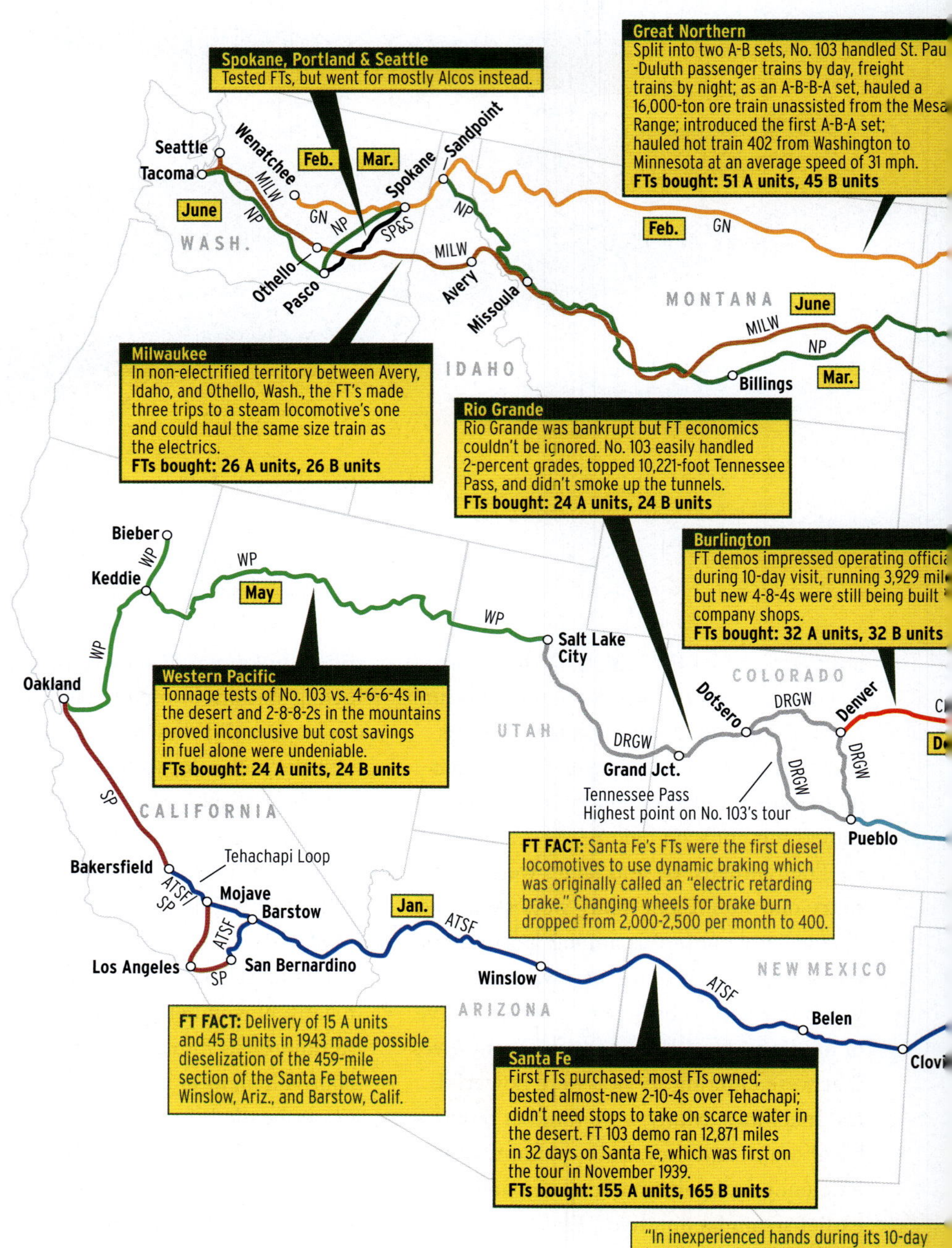

ELECTRO-MOTIVE GM ELECTRO-MOTIVE

FT DEMONSTRATOR TOUR NOVEMBER 1939 TO SEPTEMBER 1940

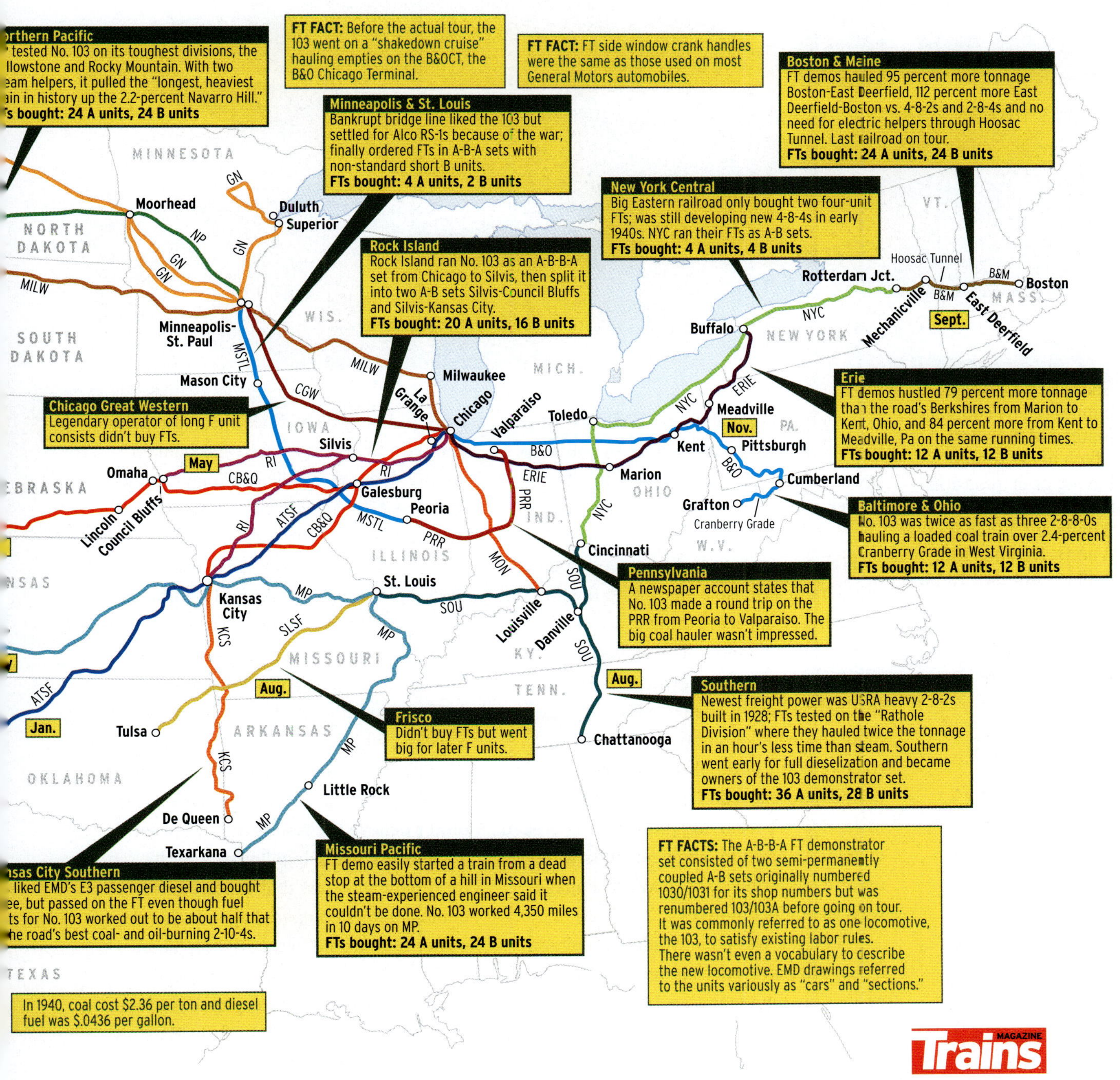

Trains MAGAZINE

Thanks to the Wallace W. Abbey family, the Center for Railroad Photography & Art and the Museum of Transportation in St. Louis

Santa Fe's FTs were connected by couplers instead of drawbars, which necessitated having grab irons and stirrups at both ends of B units and the rear of A units. Number 136, built in February 1944, also shows the dynamic brake (rooftop housing) and side number board options. *Santa Fe*

FTs were accompanied by EMD's own test (dynamometer) car and often by railroads' own dynamometer cars, enabling officials to gather and record specific data on tractive effort and other performance information.

However, railroads didn't need detailed test data or extensive analysis to quickly see several very apparent things:

• The FT would pull just about anything coupled to it, walking away with trains that had seriously challenged even large, modern steam locomotives. The starting tractive effort of the A-B-B-A set (220,000 pounds) far exceeded any steam locomotive in service. (A recurring problem was broken couplers, caused by engineers who were used to gathering slack to avoid slippage with steam locomotives.)

• The FT was equally adept at lugging a coal drag up a curving mountain grade, easing downgrade with a 16,000-ton iron ore train, or speeding across the prairie with a manifest freight train at 60 mph.

• The FT was available whenever called upon: it didn't require daily cleaning of ash pans, didn't need its flues cleaned regularly, and didn't need to have its fire banked and tended if it sat idle overnight. On its tour, the FT had zero delays because of mechanical problems.

• And the FT simply sped past the thousands of water tanks and coaling towers that lined the tracks to serve steam locomotives—all it required was a diesel fueling station every few hundred miles.

The operations and mechanical people traveling with the FT—both with EMC and the railroads—were continually impressed with its performance, and in many cases didn't believe the results they were seeing. There were many highlights from the tour; here are a few that capture how the demonstrators compared against the steam power they would eventually replace:

Santa Fe tested them on its toughest operating district: the steep grades of the Tehachapis in California. Out of Barstow, a 2-10-4 with helpers at Tehachapi could get a 2,200-ton train through in 5 hours, 55 minutes; the FT did it without helpers in 5

The demonstrator FT rolled through the winter, performing well through snow, ice, and sub-zero temperatures, as here on the Great Northern in February 1940. *Great Northern*

hours, 4 minutes. On the 25 miles of 2.55 percent grade from Caliente to Tehachapi Loop, a Southern Pacific Cab-Forward 4-8-8-2 could lift 1,350 tons up the grade in 2 hours, 15 minutes; the demonstrator pulled 1,800 tons in 1 hour, 31 minutes.

On Spokane, Portland & Seattle, the 103 and a 4-6-6-4 each took a 6,000-ton train up the railroad's 98-mile, 0.4 percent grade east of Pasco, Wash. The FT did it at a steady 26 mph; the steam locomotive averaged 10 mph.

On the Rio Grande's line from Denver westward to Moffat Tunnel, which includes a stretch of 2 percent grade, the 103 made the run with an 1,800-ton train in 5 hours, 20 minutes; the usual 2-8-8-2 on a similar train took 6 hours, 30 minutes.

The Southern Railway ran the demonstrators on its famous Rathole Division between Cincinnati, Ohio, and Chattanooga, Tenn., which featured tough grades, curves, and numerous tunnels that limited steam locomotive size. The FT took 25 percent more tonnage over the route compared to the usual USRA Heavy 2-8-2 assigned to the line, and did it in 5 hours instead of 6.

The demonstrators received 75-mph gearing, making them suitable for many passenger operations, and the B units were equipped with steam generators (they would remain a buyer option) for this contingency if railroads desired.

The Northern Pacific did just that, and not on an easy flatland route. The railroad put the 103 in charge of its top passenger train, the *North Coast Limited,* on the rugged 240-mile stretch between Livingston and Missoula, Mont., a line that included two helper districts, grades up to 2.2 percent, and 2,000 total feet of altitude change. A 4-6-6-4 could keep the *NCL* schedule with a 10-car train (12 cars with a helper); the FT pulled 17 cars on time both ways with no helper.

The Great Northern also used the FTs in passenger service, breaking them into two A-B sets and using them between St. Paul and Duluth, Minn., assigning them to

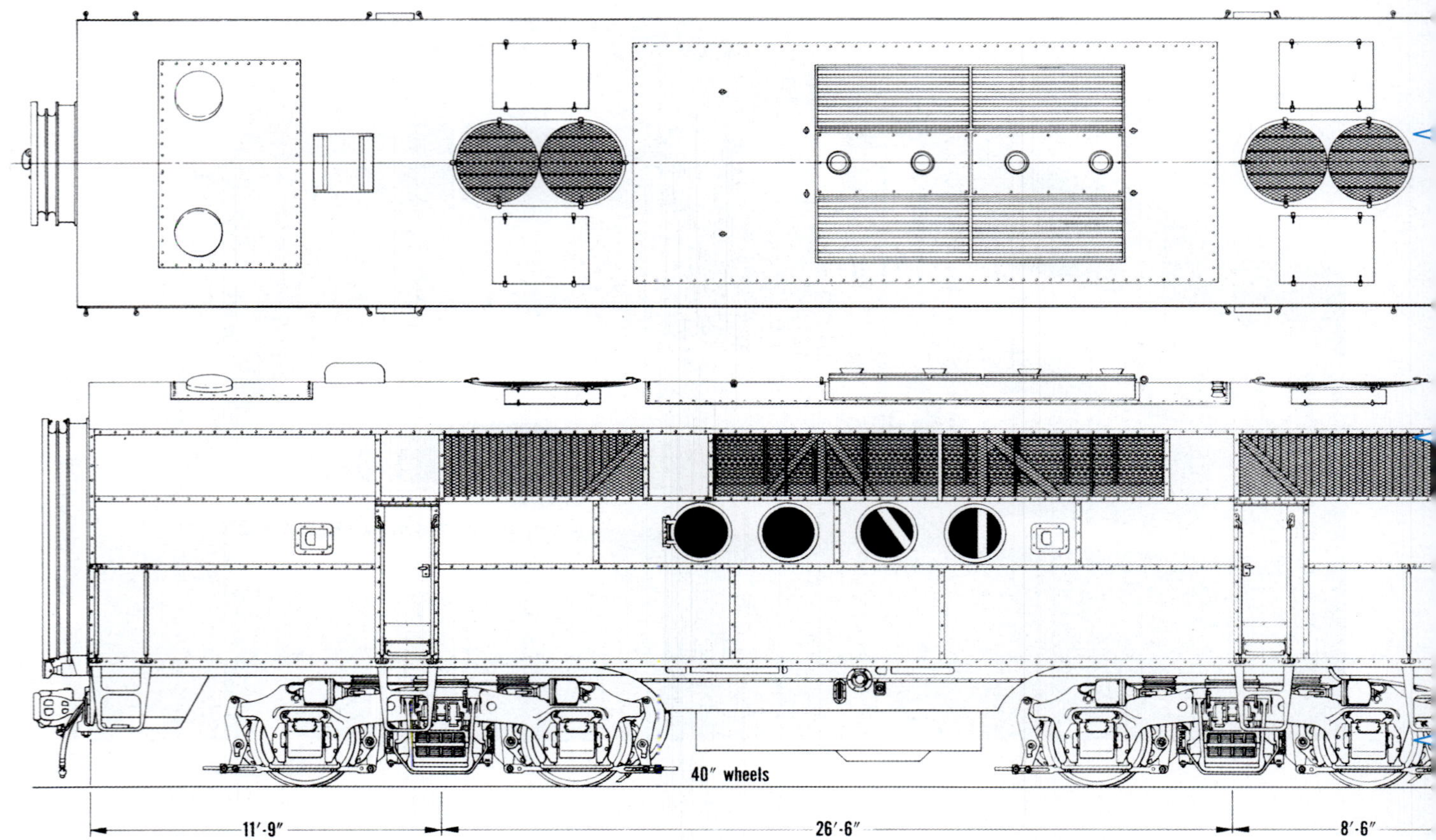

passenger runs in daytime and freight trains at night.

These runs all showed that diesels not only could equal and exceed steam locomotive performance, but that they could increase route capacity (by moving more tonnage faster, easing operating bottlenecks) and eliminate and reduce helper districts. Their high availability rate also meant it would take fewer diesels than equivalent steam engines to do the job.

By the end of the FTs' tour, the quiet publicity approach was long gone, and EMC was no longer shy about touting the diesels' performance and promoting the FTs (along with its E units and switchers), highlighting their efficiencies and why railroads should invest in this new power.

Production begins

The Santa Fe became the first railroad to put its money down for the new diesels, placing an order in September 1940. The first were delivered in December (the first A-B units of four-unit set no. 100); they officially entered revenue service on February 4, 1941. The new locomotives' first run took them 1,762 miles from Argentine Yard (Kansas City) to Los Angeles. As the railroad's initial report summarized, no. 100 did this at an average speed of 32.3 mph, pulled trains up to 3,150 tons, and replaced seven steam locomotives while passing up 28 water stops. Santa Fe was immediately sold on the FT, and over several subsequent orders became the largest FT owner with 320—and likely would have purchased more if World War II restrictions hadn't been in place.

By the time FT production ended with orders for Great Northern and Rock Island delivered in November 1945, 1,096 FTs had rolled from EMD's plant at LaGrange. A total of 23 railroads purchased FTs,

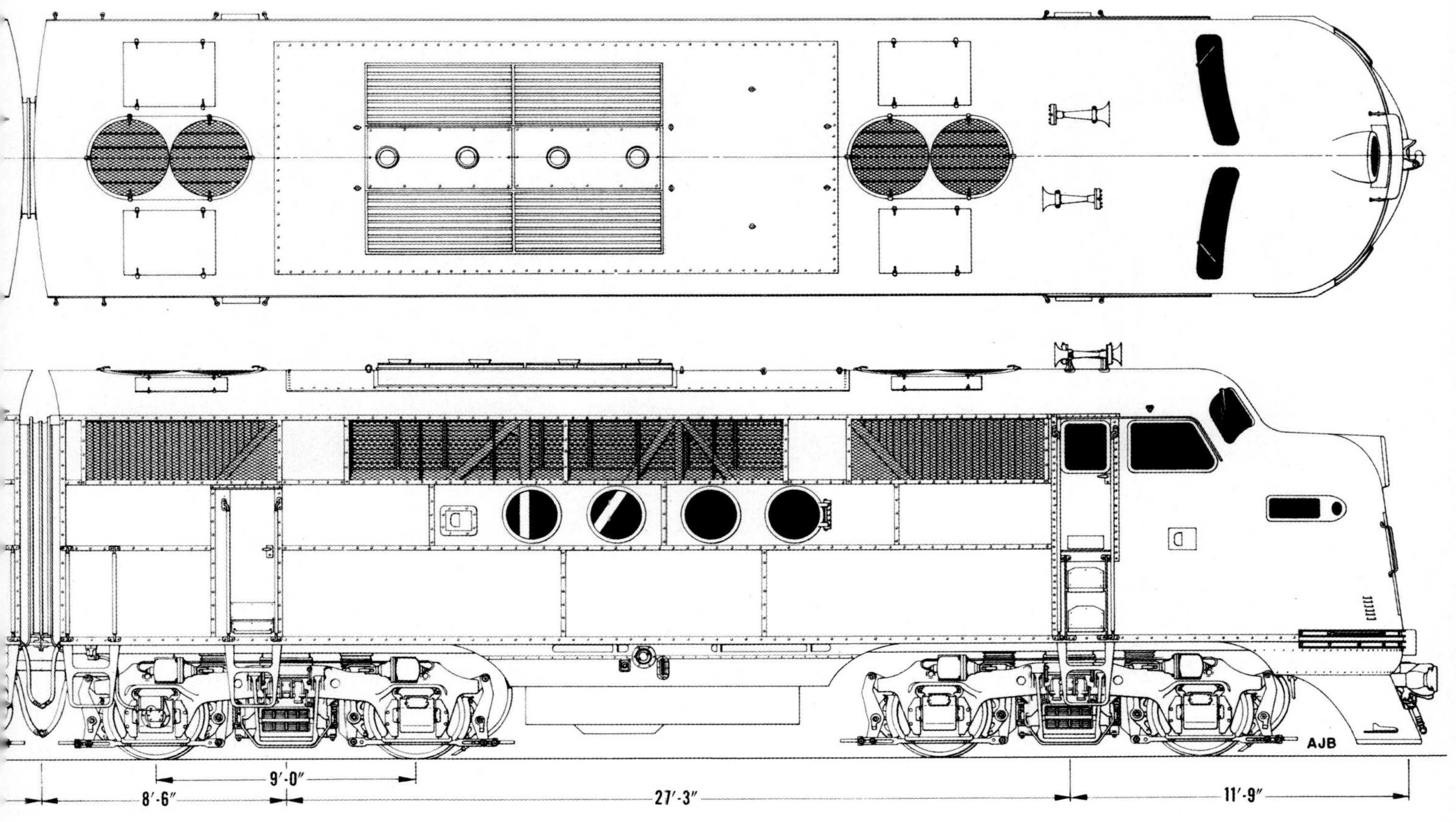

including 16 of the 20 railroads on which the demonstrators had tested. Steam's fate had been sealed: dieselization was inevitable—it was just a matter of how soon it could be accomplished.

Yes, there were other diesels that hit the rails during that period, but the FT alone effectively doomed steam locomotives. It's almost impossible to overstate the role of the FT in completely revolutionizing the railroad industry. Before 1940, many railroads acknowledged that diesels had their place as switching locomotives and in some types of passenger service. Few, however, thought diesels had a chance of supplanting steam in freight or heavy passenger service.

The FT changed that on several levels. First was reliability and availability. A steam locomotive on a 120-mile run between division points had to stop multiple times for coal and water. The diesel can just keep going past the fuel stops and the division-point stops. It's a simplified summary, but the bottom line for railroads was that steam locomotives spent a lot of time in the roundhouse: They needed constant attention from an army of laborers, machinists, and boilermakers; a diesel just needs occasional fuel. And when problems did arise, repairs were generally much simpler: instead of 8 hours in a roundhouse bay, an hour at a repair track and it was ready to go again.

This became readily apparent as railroads fully dieselized. Roundhouses disappeared; division-point engine facilities often went away, replaced by much more widely spaced (and simpler) fueling and sanding stations. Huge repair shops, with their forges and extensive machining equipment, were no longer needed—nor, unfortunately, were thousands of workers tending these positions. Although sad from a historical

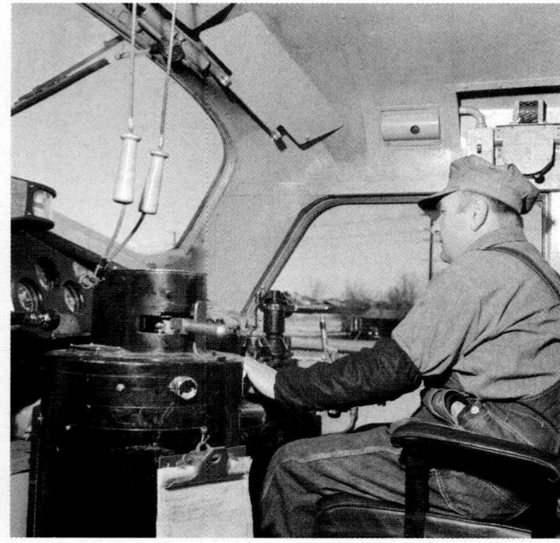

Above: Looking into a Burlington FT through the rear door, the 567A engine takes up most of the space. The radiator cores are at roof level fore and aft of the engine. *Chicago, Burlington & Quincy*

Above right: Santa Fe engineer George Bertino is in the right-hand seat of an FT, ready to lead his train out of the Winslow, Ariz., yard in March 1943. The railroad already had 78 FTs in service at that time; the line from Winslow to Barstow, Calif., would shortly be dieselized. *Jack Delano, Library of Congress*

and labor standpoint, for railroads this represented millions of dollars in savings.

Water seems like a simple thing, but it was a key reason Santa Fe and other railroads opted early for diesels. Steam locomotives use a *lot* of water (10,000 gallons or more per hour for a modern engine). Supplying this not only required frequent stops—it required thousands of wells, pumps, tanks, and towers, all of which needed maintenance. And in desert areas, it required that water be hauled in, using solid trains of tank cars; this presented an expensive operational headache.

The army of workers and extensive infrastructure network required for steam

made it an easy decision for railroads to change.

Building blocks and flexibility

A huge selling point of diesel road locomotives was the building-block principle. Individual early diesels had far less power than even an average steam locomotive (1,350 hp for a single FT compared to 3,000 hp or more for a "modern" steam locomotive). The advantage of diesels is that you can simply couple as many of them together as needed, connect them electrically, and run them as single locomotive by one engineer.

Although this wasn't fully realized yet by the FT as it would be for later F units (the FT A-B was initially considered to be a single locomotive), it still meant that the FT could be operated in A-B formation as a 2,700 hp locomotive; as an A-B-A 4,050-hp set; or as a full A-B-B-A 5,400-hp locomotive. In designing the FT, Dick Dilworth, EMC's chief engineer, planned that an A-B FT set would be equivalent to a contemporary 2-8-2 or perhaps 2-10-2, and that a full A-B-B-A set would be the equal to just about anything on the rails, including new 4-8-4s or fast articulated locomotives.

This made diesels extremely flexible; steam locomotives were inflexible. Driver size, number of powered axles, and other factors limited the types of service any given steam locomotive could perform, usually tying each steam class to a specific combination of low-speed pulling power or high-speed performance. This meant most railroads operated combinations of steam locomotives with 2-8-0, 2-8-2, 2-8-4, 4-6-2, 4-6-4, 4-8-4, 2-8-8-2, and other wheel arrangements, each for a particular service or operating division. The building-block idea virtually eliminated this need for multiple types of locomotives. The FT

Santa Fe in 1946 equipped several sets of FTs for passenger service, including no. 159. They received lower headlights and were painted in the railroad's red and silver warbonnet scheme. They would be returned to freight service by 1950 as passenger-service F3s began arriving.
Trains magazine collection

Great Northern was among railroads ordering three-unit sets of FTs, which had the shorter (by 4 feet) "FTSB" B unit. Note that the B unit lacks stirrup steps or grab irons on either end. Number 5900A was built in October 1941; it would later be renumbered 300A, 254A, and 249B.
Electro-Motive Division

was available with multiple gear ratios, which could tailor it to specific service; unlike steam, a diesel can later be regeared if needed.

Many individual steam locomotives were extremely powerful, but again, they were inflexible. Adding a second locomotive to a train ("double-heading") was certainly possible—and often done—but required a second crew, and operation took careful coordination between the crews. Diesels eliminated that.

Large steam locomotives also presented clearance issues and challenged track curvature and bridge weight limits on many lines. Diesels didn't face that—curves were no problem, and adding additional units created a longer, more powerful locomotive but didn't affect side or vertical clearance.

From a manufacturing standpoint, diesel locomotives—although more complex—could be built in assembly-line fashion, much like automobiles and trucks. Using standardized parts and components made many repairs comparatively easy, and allowed railroads to maintain parts inventories for common items such as engine components, traction motors, generators, and many smaller items—all of which were easily maintained by shop crews.

Steam locomotives were (and still are) powerful, wonderful machines, but the bottom line for railroads was that they ceased to be viable as soon as a reliable diesel-electric appeared on the market. When infrastructure and support were added to the equation, there was absolutely no contest in terms of efficiency between steam and diesel—the ultimate bottom line for railroads was that diesels were cheaper to operate and more efficient to run. Some railroads held to steam longer than others, notably major coal-haulers such as Pennsylvania, Norfolk & Western, and Chesapeake & Ohio. New road steam locomotives were still being built into 1949,

The standard FTB has a long overhang behind the rear truck, along with an end stirrup and vertical grab irons. The impracticality of having two versions of B unit bodies was not repeated on later F units. Northern Pacific no. 5400C, shown here in April 1967, is about to be traded in.
Jeff Wilson collection

Chicago & North Western no. 5401A is serviced shortly after delivery in May 1945. The green, yellow, and black diesel would be renumbered 4051A in 1947. Note the open portholes.
Chicago & North Western

Delaware, Lackawanna & Western was another railroad ordering three-unit FT sets with short FTSB B units. Dynamic-brake-equipped (note the rooftop housings) no. 601 poses for its builder's photo in April 1945.
Electro-Motive Division

and N&W and C&O both experimented with steam turbine designs, but it was too little, too late for steam.

Competition and wartime restrictions

Electro-Motive certainly had competitors—namely Alco and Baldwin in the 1930s and early 1940s, and Fairbanks-Morse starting in the mid-1940s—but they played a minor role compared to EMD's F (and E) units. The American Locomotive Co. (Alco) was the most progressive of the steam builders, having produced diesel switchers in the 1920s. It would also be a pioneer with the road-switcher concept in 1941 with the RS-1, but the company was still focused on steam production and would remain a distant second to EMD in the diesel market.

Baldwin, the largest steam builder, clung too long to the belief that steam would prevail. Although its early diesel switcher line was relatively successful, the company got into the road diesel market too late to ever be a serious competitor, and when it did, it tried too hard to stick to the steam marketing idea of custom-tailoring orders for railroads.

Lima, the other major steam builder—and a company that led innovations in steam locomotive technology with its Super-Power concepts—watched diesels pass it by. As late as 1948, Lima was still taking out ads in the trade press boldly claiming that steam would always have a place in railroading. The company built a few token switchers and road-switchers with diesel partner Hamilton, then effectively died with a 1950 merger with Baldwin.

Electro-Motive's only other serious competitor of the E and F unit era was Fairbanks-Morse, which launched its line of opposed-piston diesel switchers in 1944. The company would produce high-horsepower carbody and road switchers shortly thereafter, but would remain a minor player in the market.

Erie stuck with basic black, with yellow lettering, for its first freight-diesel road scheme. Number 700, the first of six four-unit FT sets on the railroad, was built in October 1944. *Erie*

Burlington was one of the first railroads to test demonstrator 103, and the first of 64 FTs to arrive on the property was A-B-B-A no. 100 in January 1944. In 1946, the set would be split and an F2A added to each pair to make two A-B-A sets; the FTs would be renumbered 150B-C and 151B-C. *Chicago, Burlington & Quincy*

Denver & Rio Grande Western no. 540 was delivered in January 1942. As with Santa Fe, Rio Grande had its FTs all equipped with couplers (note stirrups and grab irons at the ends of A units and both ends of Bs, and the extra porthole on the B at right). The dynamic brake housings have the intermediate curved sides. Note the similarity in the striping to the demonstrator FTs. *Denver & Rio Grande Western*

The bottom line was that EMD dominated the road-diesel market, selling 70 percent of the diesels that replaced steam.

World War II played a major role in diesel locomotive development, with U.S. involvement in the war starting just a year after FT production began. The War Production Board allowed Electro-Motive—which in January 1941 had officially become the Electro-Motive Division of GM, or EMD—to continue building FTs during World War II. The WPB had to approve orders; there was a brief hiatus from December 1942 to February 1943 as EMD was also building engines for Navy vessels. Alco and Baldwin were only allowed to build diesel switching locomotives, and then only at WPB discretion. This gave EMD a jump (three years and almost 1,000 locomotives) in working out bugs and refining its FTs. (See "War Production Board and Antitrust Hearings" on page 72).

As the war ended and EMD and other builders began ramping up production to meet the tremendous demands of railroads for new locomotives, the company was in excellent shape to continue dominating the market.

FT design

The FT was built under the direction of EMC's chief designer, Richard M. (Dick) Dilworth. In designing the FT, Dilworth and EMC took all that it had learned since its formation in the 1920s, from its early gasoline-powered motor cars to switchers to the first passenger locomotives. The emergence of the stand-alone E unit and off-the-shelf, assembly-line production techniques of the E3 and E6 (and their growing popularity by 1939) showed that the FT should be a mass-produced design that could, with minimal options, be adaptable for use in all types of freight service and appeal to virtually any railroad.

The streamliner power cars of the mid-1930s and the early Es had allowed EMC to work out many issues and problems, notably replacing the troublesome 201A diesel with the more-reliable 567 engine and producing its own electrical equipment instead of relying on General Electric and other outside vendors.

The basic body design followed that of the contemporary E6: The FT was given a streamlined carbody with side truss framework that enabled a lighter platform

This rooftop view of Santa Fe FTs provides a good look at the original square-sided dynamic brake housings. *Santa Fe*

On FTs without dynamic brakes, the roofline was fairly smooth, with just the four centered exhaust stacks protruding upward. Note the two pairs of recessed radiator fans, each with a screen-covered round opening. This is a Seaboard Air Line FT in 1963. *J. Parker Lamb*

FT PRODUCTION

Railroad	A units	B units	Dates Built
AT&SF	155	165	12/40-8/45
ACL	24	24	9/43-12/44
B&O	12	12	8/42-10/43
B&M	24	24	9/43-11/44
C&NW	4	4	5/45
CB&Q	32	32	12/43-9/44
CRI&P	20	16	4/44-11/45
DL&W	12	8	5/43-10/44
D&RGW	24	24	1/42-10/44
Erie	12	12	10/44-11/44
GN	51	45	12/43-11/45
LV	4	4	1/45
MILW	26	26	10/41-7/45
M&StL	4	2	4/45
MP	12	12	11/43-7/45
NYC	4	4	6/44
NYO&W	9	9	5/45
NP	22	22	2/44-1/45
RDG	10	10	1/45-2/45
SAL	22	22	6/42-10/44
SSW	10	10	6/44-6/45
SOU	38	30	5/41-8/45
WP	24	24	11/41-11/44

Western Pacific FT no. 902 leads an eastbound perishable freight in the early 1940s. The locomotive, built in December 1941, has dynamic brake housings with curved sides. *Western Pacific*

and underframe. The FT was shorter than an E: 47'-6" for an A unit, compared to 71'-1" for a contemporary E6, made possible by powering it with a single engine, a 16-cylinder version of the 567 rated at 1,350 hp.

The body had a less-slanted ("bulldog") nose, with an 80-degree angle instead of the 70-degree version of early E units. This simplified construction and allowed a shorter frame, and would be used on all subsequent Fs and Es. A nose access door was added; number boards were located on each side where the nose curve started.

The sides used the same construction technique as the E, with metal-covered plywood panels held by batten strips. The FT was easily identified from later Fs by its group of four side portholes located horizontally along the middle of each side. One porthole in each group was hinged to open. The top of each side had screen-covered openings for air intakes, with truss framing visible behind them. A 1,200-gallon fuel tank was suspended from the frame between the trucks.

On the roof were screened openings for two pairs of radiator fans (two on a forward panel, two toward the rear), as the radiator was divided and placed fore and aft of the engine at ceiling level. Four exhaust stacks were directly above the engine, centered on the roof between the fans. Locomotives equipped with dynamic brakes (more on those in a bit) had the resistor grids in a housing between the fans.

The FT demonstrators used the original 567U engine, which had a cast-steel top deck in the crankcase; production models had the upgraded 567V, which substituted

With white extra flags flying, a matched set of Western Pacific FTs rolls its last miles along the Humboldt River near Elko, Nev., in October 1964. The rooftop number boards were a WP modification. *Gordon Glattenberg*

a fabricated (welded) deck (the upgraded engines had first appeared in the E6). The engine turned a single D8 generator, which powered the four D7 traction motors (one on each axle). The engine would be upgraded again in 1943, to the 567A. This engine maintained the same horsepower rating, but with changes to the exhaust outlet and manifold for better cooling and reliability.

The FT rode on four axles—a pair of two-axle, four-wheel trucks, with all axles powered—compared to the six-axle E units, giving it a B-B wheel arrangement. The slower speeds of freight service and lighter body weight didn't require the additional stability and ride quality offered by six-wheel trucks, and eliminating the idler axles (the center axle of each E unit truck) put the full weight of the locomotive upon the driving wheels, increasing pulling power.

The trucks were an important part of the FT design. Most four-wheel switcher and freight locomotives to that time rode on variations of what would become known as the AAR Type B road truck. However, EMC designer Martin Blomberg designed an all-new truck based on his successful six-wheel A1A (two outside powered axles with a middle idler axle) trucks that he had designed for E units.

Blomberg's four-wheel "F" design had two powered axles with 40"-diameter wheels (compared to 36" on E units), and a 9'-0" wheelbase. The use of outside swing hangers, a center leaf spring, journal-box coil springs, and elliptic bolster springs (plus roller-bearing journals) made the truck more stable with a better, smoother ride compared to earlier four-wheel trucks.

With minor modifications and upgrades, the Blomberg truck was used under all F units until production ended in the late 1950s, and versions were used on Electro-Motive's four-axle road switchers until the 1990s.

As with EMC's passenger E units, railroads could order FTs in several gear ratio combinations, opting for more tractive effort at lower minimum speeds or faster maximum speed. Available gear ratios were 65:12 (45 mph maximum), 62:15 (65 mph), 61:16 (70 mph), 59:18 (80 mph), 58:19 (89 mph), and 57:20 (95 mph). Most railroads opted for 62:15 and some flatland roads 61:16; a few chose 65:12 for locomotives destined for helper service (Lackawanna) or slow-speed main lines (New York, Ontario & Western). Santa Fe

WAR PRODUCTION BOARD AND ANTI-TRUST HEARINGS

Locomotive production during World War II presented a complicated situation. The War Production Board (WPB) regulated materials critical to the war effort. Railroads were vital for transporting materials (military and consumer), troops, and other passengers, so keeping them furnished with enough locomotives to do their jobs was extremely important.

By 1942, FT sales were booming, and many railroads wanted new diesel locomotives, not steam. However, traditional steam manufacturers were allowed to continue building steam locomotives because their plants weren't easily converted to other military use, and steam locomotives used fewer critical materials.

Diesel engines were needed for Navy vessels (and EMD had a large Navy contract), limiting the number of engines available for locomotives. Other materials required for diesel locomotives (such as copper for wiring) were in high demand for military items. Also, coal for steam locomotives was plentiful; petroleum was in high demand overseas for airplanes, ships, and vehicles, with consumer rationing in place.

Thus the WPB allowed EMD, as a diesel-only builder with the only successful road-freight diesel on the market, to continue building FTs (with the WPB deciding which railroads got them, and how many), but not switchers or passenger locomotives. Traditional steam manufacturers Alco and Baldwin had to continue building steam locomotives along with a limited number of diesel switchers.

This led to many accusations over the years of EMD getting a large, unfair advantage in being allowed to refine its already-successful freight locomotive while its competitors were limited to switchers.

It's certainly a valid point that EMD took advantage of this time, but it's also overblown when considering where the company stood at the start of the war, when it was technologically already far ahead of its competition. Another valid point is that EMD certainly didn't sell as many locomotives as it would have had WPB restrictions not been in place.

The accusations were strong enough that EMD was one of the targets of a federal anti-trust hearing involving GM in the mid-1950s. Testimony from GM in its defense pointed out that EMD's advantage came before the war, when it was developing advanced diesel-electric technology and selling more locomotives than its competitors while traditional steam builders ignored diesels or treated them as a secondary production operation. Electro-Motive noted that as late as 1946 all three major steam builders (Baldwin, Alco, and Lima) were introducing new steam locomotives that were being advertised as being able to out-perform diesels (as late as 1949 in Lima's case). One GM official during testimony said, "Actually, the greatest competitive advantage the Electro-Motive Division of General Motors had was the attitude of its competitors."

The EMD competitors' accusation was officially that "GM received an unfair advantage during World War II under War Production Board allocations." However, the GM official said, "when World War II started, GM was the only company with a proven freight locomotive in production. For this reason, we were confined to road freight power and all others were limited to switcher power."

had one set regeared to 57:20 for high-speed passenger service; the railroad would later opt for similar gearing for its passenger-service F3s and F7s.

The FT was built based on the A-B principle; the intent was that the A and B units (which were initially called "sections") were the forward and rear parts of the same locomotive—not two separate locomotives—connected semipermanently by drawbars. The B units were not meant to be interchangeable (they did not have batteries), and relied on their A units for control. This meant a railroad could run an A-B by itself, couple two sets back to back, or order an A-B-A set.

This was in large part because of early reaction by railroad operating unions, which were insisting that separate locomotives should each have operating crews (like double-headed steam locomotives)—which would, of course, negate much of

Left: Seaboard Air Line FT 4011 leads a cement train in the 1940s. Built in November 1943, it has the insert-style headlight with the protruding rim.
Seaboard Air Line

Below: The bankrupt New York, Ontario & Western dieselized its mainline freight operations with nine A-B sets of FTs that arrived in May 1945; a set is shown here in September 1946. The improved economical operations weren't enough to save the railroad, which ceased operations in March 1957.
Union Switch & Signal

COLORFUL CARDS

Electro-Motive's corporate promotional department took advantage of the public's interest in new diesels by issuing postcard-sized cards of their new products. The front of each card featured an artist's rendering of an E or F unit locomotive in color; the back included a description of the locomotive along with data such as dimensions and weight. This artwork was also released in poster size, and often given to officers of railroads. The artwork was usually done prior to the locomotives being completed, so the artwork sometimes didn't quite match what was actually on the real thing. These items are collectible, and can often be found at railroad shows and online dealers.

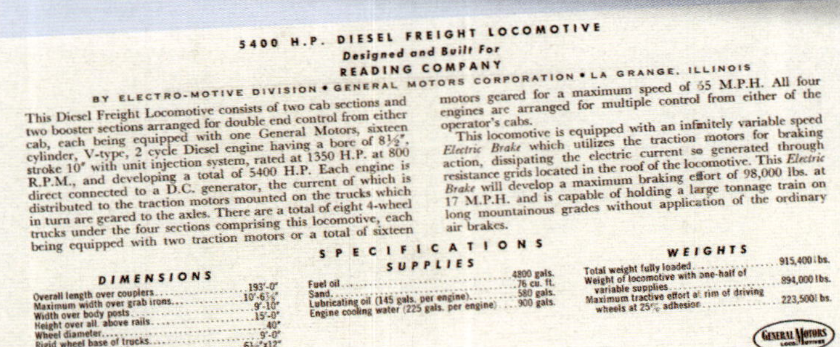

5400 H.P. DIESEL FREIGHT LOCOMOTIVE
Designed and Built For
READING COMPANY
BY ELECTRO-MOTIVE DIVISION • GENERAL MOTORS CORPORATION • LA GRANGE, ILLINOIS

This Diesel Freight Locomotive consists of two cab sections and two booster sections arranged for double end control from either cab, each being equipped with one General Motors, sixteen cylinder, V-type, 2 cycle Diesel engine having a bore of 8½", stroke 10" with unit injection system, rated at 1350 H.P. at 800 R.P.M., and developing a total of 5400 H.P. Each engine is direct connected to a D.C. generator, the current of which is distributed to the traction motors mounted on the trucks which in turn are geared to the axles. There are a total of eight 4-wheel trucks under the four sections comprising this locomotive, each being equipped with two traction motors or a total of sixteen motors geared for a maximum speed of 65 M.P.H. All four engines are arranged for multiple control from either of the operator's cabs.

This locomotive is equipped with an infinitely variable speed *Electric Brake* which utilizes the traction motors for braking action, dissipating the electric current so generated through resistance grids located in the roof of the locomotive. This *Electric Brake* will develop a maximum braking effort of 98,000 lbs. at 17 M.P.H. and is capable of holding a large tonnage train on long mountainous grades without application of the ordinary air brakes.

SPECIFICATIONS

DIMENSIONS

Overall length over couplers .... 193'-0"
Maximum width over grab irons .... 10'-6⅜"
Width over body posts .... 9'-10"
Height over all above rails .... 15'-0"
Wheel diameter .... 40"
Rigid wheel base of trucks .... 9'-0"
Roller bearing journals .... 6½"x12"
Truck swing designed for 21° curve or 274-foot radius
Distance between truck centers on cab section .... 27'-3"
Distance between truck centers on booster section 26'-6"

SUPPLIES

Fuel oil .... 4800 gals.
Sand .... 76 cu. ft.
Lubricating oil (145 gals. per engine) .... 580 gals.
Engine cooling water (225 gals. per engine) .... 900 gals.

WEIGHTS

Total weight fully loaded .... 915,400 lbs.
Weight of locomotive with one-half of variable supplies .... 894,000 lbs.
Maximum tractive effort at rim of driving wheels at 25% adhesion .... 223,500 lbs.

GENERAL MOTORS LOCOMOTIVES

the building-block savings of diesels. This remained a factor in some areas for several years, but by the mid-1940s, wartime exemptions and then negotiations with the Brotherhoods had established that individual diesels connected electrically could be operated by a single crew.

This also led to many numbering variations among carbody locomotives on A and B units. An early common practice

Northern Pacific was the last Class 1 railroad to operate FTs. Here no. 5403A leads a freight at Sumas, Wash., in June 1968. An FT A-B set brackets each end of this six-F-unit consist. The NP added nose grab irons and lift rings and a lower twin-beam headlight to its FT A units. *J. David Ingles*

was to assign one number the entire set (two, three, or four units). These were typically sublettered for both operational and maintenance reasons, usually by A, B, C, and D, but Santa Fe, for example, numbered its Fs with L (for lead), A, B, and C. This meant many variations, with A units sometimes sublettered A, C, D, or L; B units might be A, B, or C. And some railroads later sublettered B units further; Chicago Great Western, famous for running long sets of F units, had F3 B units sublettered E, F, and G. These subletters sometimes appeared in number boards (of A units) or with large unit numbers on the bodies; they were sometimes shown only in small size (an inch or two in height) beneath the unit numbers or on the side frame or below the cab.

Some railroads foresaw the flexibility that individual units would provide and

Minneapolis & St. Louis FT no. 545 leads time freight No. 20 from Minneapolis to Peoria as it approaches Oskaloosa, Iowa, around 1950. The railroad bought two three-unit sets of FTs with short (FTSB) B units in April 1945. The railroad was known for numbering its diesels based on their delivery dates. *Bob Milner*

ordered their FTs with couplers instead of drawbars—notably Santa Fe, starting with the very first order. This was not an easy alteration because of the frame and drawbar design, but Electro-Motive did it for what it hoped would be a good customer. On these B units, batteries were added and a simple hostler control stand was built in on one end (allowing the B to be moved on its own). These can be spotted by an extra porthole on the engineer's side of the B, hinged to open so the hostler could look out.

Over the years, some railroads split their FTs, swapping the drawbars for couplers (which was not a simple process)—see the Missouri Pacific FT at the top of page 77—but most ran their entire careers matched in A-B sets as they were built. The true building-block idea of individual units wouldn't come until F2s and F3s, which

Milwaukee Road added lower signal lights to the bottom of the nose doors on its FTs, as on no. 37, shown here getting serviced in April 1946. The black plate on the right of the front number board covers the "A" or "D" in the number; the plate is removed when the locomotive is split into A-B sets. *Milwaukee Road*

Missouri Pacific FT no. 502 leads a pair of B units on a freight train. The lead A-B is drawbar-connected, while the trailing B unit has couplers at each end. *C.E. Winters; Louis A. Marre collection*

had couplers on both ends of B units as the standard option.

Variations and details

The FT B unit bodies varied in length based on whether they were built as part of an A-B set or part of an A-B-A set. The standard (FTB) body was very distinctive, with a long overhang behind the rear truck (a look not repeated on later F units). The Bs in A-B-A sets were shorter (43'-10" compared to 48'-1"), and were designated FTSB. They can be spotted by their lack of a rear overhang.

Stirrup steps and vertical grab irons—required at each end of a locomotive—were initially placed only on the rear of each B unit in A-B sets: there was no grab/stirrup at the front of the B or the rear of the A, since the locomotives were meant to be kept together. On FTSBs there were no end grabs/stirrups on either end (nor on the rear of either A of the A-B-A set), again, as the units were designed to stay together.

Coupler-equipped B units (and rear As) had stirrups and grabs on the ends to meet safety regulations. Also, if drawbar-connected sets were subsequently separated and given couplers, steps and grab irons were added. See the Santa Fe photos and the Rio Grande A unit on page 68 for examples. The spacing between drawbar-connected units was also tighter than on coupler-connected engines.

Steam generators were an option on FTs, with the boiler located at the rear of the B unit. They can be spotted by the stack and vent on the rear-most roof hatch. Space was tight in the carbody, so there wasn't much room for a water tank (600 gallons was standard). Railroads ordering at least some FTs with steam generators included Atlantic Coast Line, Boston & Maine, Great Northern, Northern Pacific, Rio Grande, Southern, and Western Pacific; Santa Fe added them later on some locomotives.

Other options included headlights; as with E units, lower headlights became a common option on FT and later F units. Some had a separate reflector insert on the upper headlight, resulting in a lip around the headlight (see the Seaboard engines on

Six-year-old no. 907 (formerly 905A) leads an A-B-B set of FTs on St. Louis Southwestern (Cotton Belt) Train 126 at Tyler, Texas, in 1950. Cotton Belt had begun to separate its drawbar-equipped FT sets by this time; the trailing FT is equipped with couplers on both ends.
R.S. Plummer

pages 69 and 73). Some were built with illuminated number panels centered on the sides. Added grab irons above the cab windows and on the nose, along with radio antennas, were often added after the FTs were placed in service.

All FTs were equipped for multiple-unit (MU) operation, but as-built the connections were only located at the rear of the A unit and both ends of B units (there was no provision for adding additional B units to an A-B-B-A locomotive). A few railroads added nose MU connections (see the Rio Grande engine on page 83), but it was rare for FTs.

Dynamic braking

The FT was the first diesel-electric to offer what became known as dynamic braking as an added railroad option. The system was based on the regenerative braking systems of electric locomotives, a type of locomotive braking that used the traction motors as generators to provide rolling resistance, with the resulting electricity they produced put back into the overhead wire. With the FT (and subsequent diesels), the difference was that electricity made by the motors was sent to large banks of resistors on the locomotive.

To engage the dynamic brakes, the engineer threw a switch that energized the traction motor fields, turning them into generators. This provides a great deal of resistance to turning—the axles have to work hard to turn against the force of the motors, which are now generators. The electricity they create is sent to large banks of resistors on the roof—picture a large

Rock Island FT no. 99 was built in April 1944. The Rock, which owned 36 FTs, would find four-unit sets too powerful and in 1946 bought a dozen F2As, matching each to an FT A-B set. *Rock Island*

toaster—and dissipated as heat.

Dynamic braking was a revolutionary feature, especially for railroads operating in mountainous areas with heavy trains. It became possible for many trains to keep their speed in control strictly with dynamic braking, or with minimal assistance from the standard automatic (air) brakes. This provided better train control, a higher level of safety in operations, and saved a significant amount of wear on brake shoes and wheels, which otherwise had to endure the tremendous heat of being applied for a long period of time.

A common question is why the resistors were needed. The answer is that without a load on the generators (traction motors), there would be no rolling resistance; the circuit has to be closed, and thus the electricity has to be used—hence the resistor grid. The resistors become extremely hot during operation, so additional fans are required to cool the grid; the fans cooling the traction motors also have to have enough capacity to keep their temperature within operating limits as well.

The Santa Fe opted for dynamic brakes from their first production FT order onward, and was very pleased with their operation; many subsequent railroads also chose them. The initial braking system offered was limited; engineers had just two settings to choose from to apply more or less braking. In late 1941 this system was improved with a controller that allowed zero to full dynamic braking, providing much better control over the brakes. Dynamic brakes would become an option for all later F units,

Southern Railway FT no. 6102 (with B units 6154, 6155, and A unit 6103) was technically owned by subsidiary Cincinnati, New Orleans & Texas Pacific. It was built in December 1943. *Trains magazine collection*

E8 and E9 passenger diesels, and road-switchers of EMD and other manufacturers.

Locomotives equipped with dynamic brakes were easy to spot, with the resistor grids located in large, boxy housings centered on the roof on either side of the exhaust stacks. The shape of these housings changed during production. The early boxy (vertical-sided) housing in mid-production gave way to curved sides (see the Western Pacific FTs on page 70); however, the change affected cooling, so they were changed back to vertical sides before FT production ended. Some of these had additional boxes fore and aft (see the photo of the New York Central FTs on the opposite page).

Continued evolution

The FT proved itself in varied service, operating across the country, from Maine (Boston & Maine, with 48 FTs) to Florida (Atlantic Coast Line, 48) to California (Santa Fe, 320) and almost every state in between. They were at their best on priority mainline through freights, which is where they spent most of their working careers.

The largest FT fleet by far was Santa Fe's, but they were represented well on other transcontinentals with varied line

New York Central rostered just eight FTs: four A-B sets acquired in June 1944. They had dynamic brakes (the late style of rooftop housing with additional boxes fore and aft) and wore a simple black scheme. Here A-B set 1601/2401 rest in the late 1940s.
Trains magazine collection

profiles including Great Northern (96), Milwaukee Road (52), and Northern Pacific (44); on granger railroads such as Burlington (64), Rock Island (36), Missouri Pacific (24), and St. Louis Southwestern (20); on Western mountain railroads such as Rio Grande (48) and Western Pacific (48); and in the Northeast on Lackawanna (24), Erie (24), and Reading (20).

Were the FTs perfect? Certainly not. Many internal mechanical features, such as belt-driven cooling fans, were maintenance headaches. Manually controlled cooling fans, manual transition, early hard-wired electrical gear, and other items could cause operational problems. And although assembly line techniques were used during construction, they weren't efficient enough—even with a mid-production revision in assembly steps that saved hundreds of hours per unit in construction time, they simply took too long to build.

The FT was not well-suited to local freight (way freight) service, branchline trains, industrial work, or mainline freights where a great deal of en route switching was done. Their rear visibility was limited, making back-and-forth (switching) operations challenging (which is why road-switcher designs eventually dominated the market). And when they were eventually bumped from their original assignments by newer diesels, they were ill-suited for other types of service, and their early technology and construction did not lend them to rebuilding.

As World War II come to a close and railroads were poised to invest heavily in new locomotives, EMD knew it was time to introduce new locomotive designs for both its passenger E (see Chapter 4) and freight F units. Goals were to improve efficiency in assembly with modular construction and more common components among models, to take advantage of upgraded technology to provide more power per unit, and to make the locomotives more reliable and efficient. The result for EMD would be a complete redesign in the transitional F2, with upgraded power in a new locomotive emerging in the even-more popular F3 and F7 (see Chapter 5).

The FT was a resounding success and proved to be everything railroads had hoped for and needed. Barring wrecks, almost all of them had long, successful service lives. Most ran into the late 1950s, but as new, more-powerful road switchers became available from the late 1950s into the 1960s, the FTs became the first diesels to become candidates for trading in—a program strongly encouraged by EMD to keep new diesels going out the door—making them the first diesel locomotives to be replaced by new diesels.

As FT production drew to a close in 1945, Class 1 railroads operated 3,816 diesels and 38,853 steam locomotives. Looking at those numbers, it would seem that steam still had a strong hold on

It's evening at Mechanicville, N.Y., as Boston & Maine FT 4221 A-B and an F2 prepare to depart with Train MB-6 for Boston in the mid-1950s. Boston & Maine would trade in all 48 of its FTs to EMD in 1957 on an order for GP9s. *Jim Shaughnessy*

American railroads, but that was not the case. Many of those steam locomotives were old and worn out, having worked hard pulling record levels of traffic during World War II. Railroads were working to replace them as fast as possible, and their replacements would be diesels.

Longtime *Trains* magazine editor David P. Morgan in 1972 summed up the success of the FT and other early diesels overtaking steam as "giving the railroads an opportunity to concentrate their energies on running trains," not on maintaining, watering, cleaning, and caring for steam locomotives. The FT allowed railroads to take a locomotive, plug it into just about any situation, and with minimal fuss, allow it to do its job. This job would be continued by the F2 and F3, as Chapter 5 will show.

Rio Grande FT 5404 and three sisters are at Galesburg, Ill., on the Burlington, working their way eastward on their final trip to EMD as trade-in material on February 25, 1962. The D&RGW modified its FTs with large number boxes, a lower signal light in the nose door, nose MU capability (socket to the right of the upper headlight), and additional nose and windshield grab irons. *J. David Ingles*

CHAPTER 4

POST-WAR PASSENGER BOOM

THE E7, E8, AND E9 DIESELIZED PASSENGER TRAINS

An Illinois Central E8 pauses at Springfield, Ill., in April 1966. Built in April 1952, no. 4026 was one of the last E8s built. *Craig Willett*

As World War II began drawing to a close, locomotive production ramped up as wartime restrictions were eased and removed. American railroads had carried record amounts of both freight and passengers, and equipment was old and worn out. Railroads began buying diesel locomotives as fast as manufacturers could build them.

Passenger equipment had been especially heavily taxed, with only steam locomotives and the few prewar diesels to pull them. Railroads began ordering not only new passenger diesel locomotives, but entire train sets to replace older equipment, continuing the move to lightweight, streamlined equipment that had begun before the war. The public was now able to travel without restrictions, and people were taking advantage in record numbers.

Electro-Motive had turned out its last E6 passenger diesel in September 1942, when War Production Board restrictions ended their manufacture. However, EMD had been allowed to continue building its FT freight diesel through most of the war. Although both had been successful, by 1944 EMD had begun planning for new E and F unit models to replace them.

Electro-Motive had learned a lot about locomotive production in the three previous years, including feedback from railroads and its in-factory experiences. It was ready to apply the lessons learned—including what needed improvement along with what worked well—with the upgraded locomotives.

A key goal with the new locomotives was streamlining the manufacturing process, doing as many tasks in subassemblies and using modular components whenever possible to cut down final assembly time. Earlier diesels (including the E6 and early FTs) were too heavily "stick-built," as some described, with too many assembly steps. This had been improved during FT production but needed more refinement. Along with this was a goal to combine components among models as much as possible, so more of the same parts would be interchangeable among freight, passenger, and switching locomotives, simplifying construction and making parts inventory easier and more economical for railroads.

The results of the redesign were the F2 and F3 freight diesel (see Chapter 5) and the E7 passenger diesel.

Pere Marquette no. 103, built in April 1947, served the railroad for just two months until PM was merged into Chesapeake & Ohio in June of that year. It would be among C&O's first diesels. The large diagonal number boxes and lower headlight were both buyer options.
Electro-Motive Division

EMD's most-popular passenger diesel: the E7

The first production E7 emerged from LaGrange in March 1945, and the E7 would become the most-popular passenger diesel ever built. More than 500 would be purchased by U.S. railroads by the time production ended in early 1949. There was no demonstrator E7—none was needed, as railroads were lined up to buy them as fast as EMD could build them.

Mechanically the E7 was similar to the E6, powered by two 12-cylinder diesel engines, but these were the upgraded 567A design first used in the FT in 1943 (modifications to the exhaust outlet and manifold provided better cooling and reliability compared to the original 567). The E7 was still rated at 2,000 hp like the E6. It still used the D4 generator and D7 traction motors of the E6, but during production the traction motors were upgraded to the D17 model.

Visually, the most striking change was

Gulf, Mobile & Ohio E7 no. 103 leads an F3 and another E7 on the point of Train 1, *The Limited,* at LeMont, Ill., on December 30, 1966. The E7 became EMD's best-selling passenger diesel. The GM&O had seven (all A units) acquired via merger from the Alton.
Tom Hoffman

E7 CUTAWAY VIEW

1. Engine no. 1 (12-567A)
2. Engine no. 2 (12-567A)
3. Main generators
4. Load regulators
5. Traction motors
6. Radiators (shown on engine no. 1 only)
7. Coolant tanks
8. Engine cooling fan
9. Lube oil filter tank
10. Steam generator water tank
11. Fuel oil tank
12. Truck (Blomberg A1A)
13. Steam generator
14. Air compressor

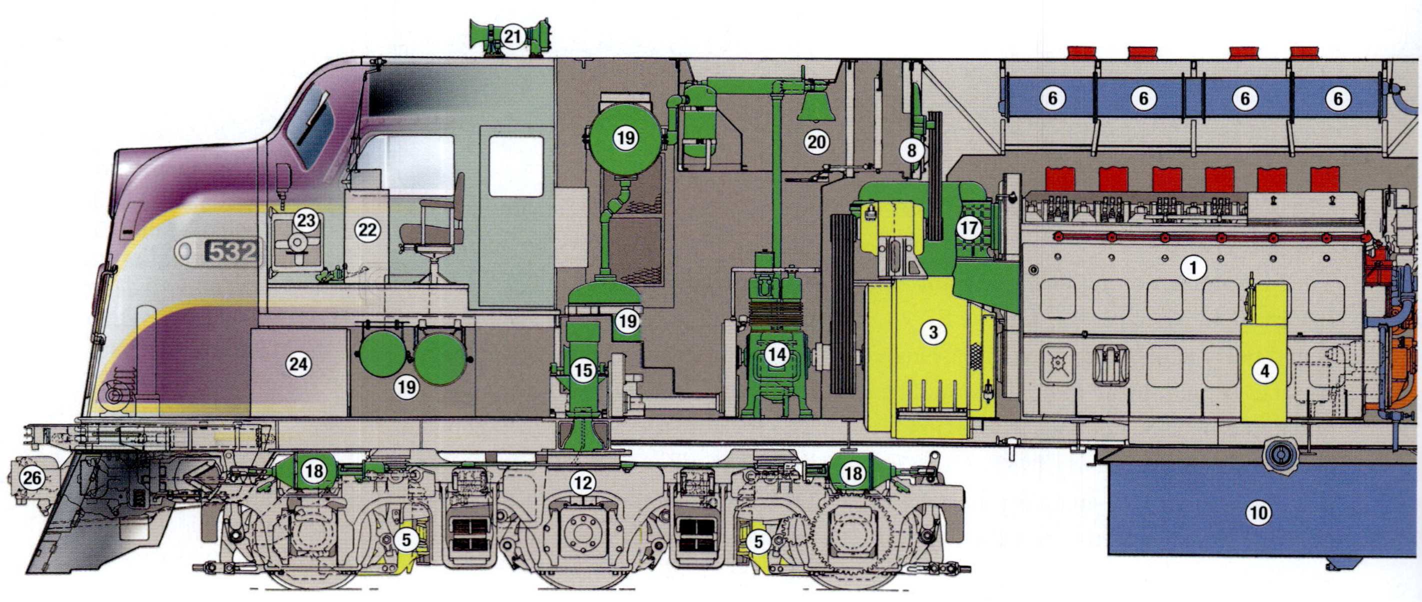

Chicago, Burlington & Quincy E7 no. 9925A leads three other Es on westbound Train 11, the combined *Kansas City Zephyr* and *Nebraska Zephyr*, west of Wyanet, Ill., in October 1966. Number 9925A is an early E7, built in November 1945. The Burlington would eventually roster 44 E7As, built through March 1949. *Craig Willett*

15. Traction motor blower
16. Lube oil cooler
17. Engine Roots blower
18. Brake cylinders
19. Air reservoirs
20. Bell
21. Horns
22. Operator's controls
23. Cab heater
24. Battery box
25. Exhaust manifold (shown on engine no. 2 only)
26. Couplers

Key: Yellow = electrical; Blue = water/cooling; Orange = lube oil system; Red = fuel/exhaust; Green = air brakes/fans

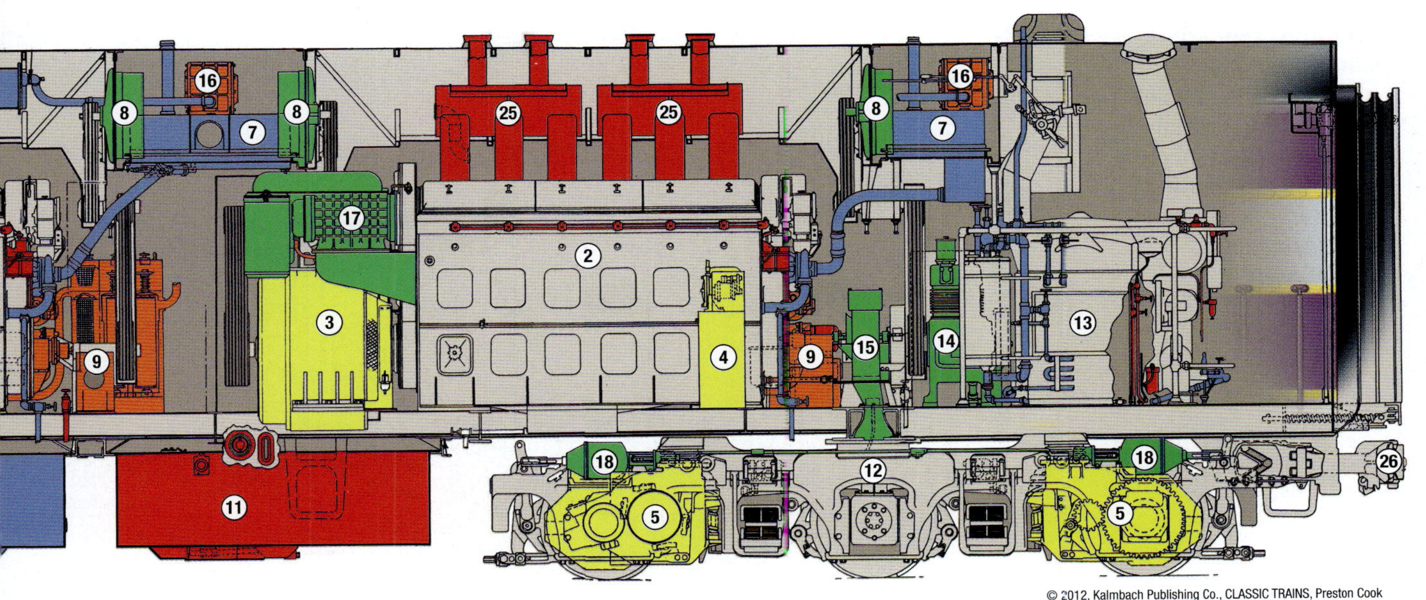

Great Northern E7 no. 512, built in August 1947, has the alternate screened access door behind the cab door. It also has ladder grabs on the nose, along with grab irons above the window and a lower headlight. The railroad used its 13 E7s mainly on regional and short-haul trains, preferring F units for transcontinental streamliners.
Great Northern

ELECTRO-MOTIVE DIVISION E7A

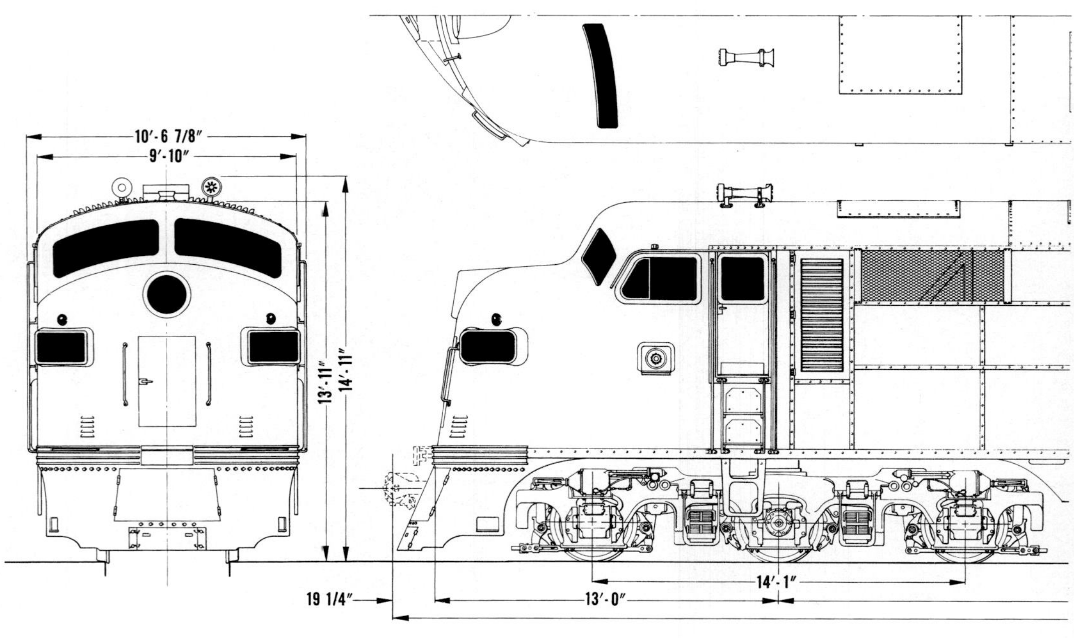

Alton acquired seven E7As in 1945 and 1946, just before its merger into Gulf, Mobile & Ohio in 1947. Here two of them lead the *Abe Lincoln* at Joliet, Ill., in 1947.
J. David Ingles collection

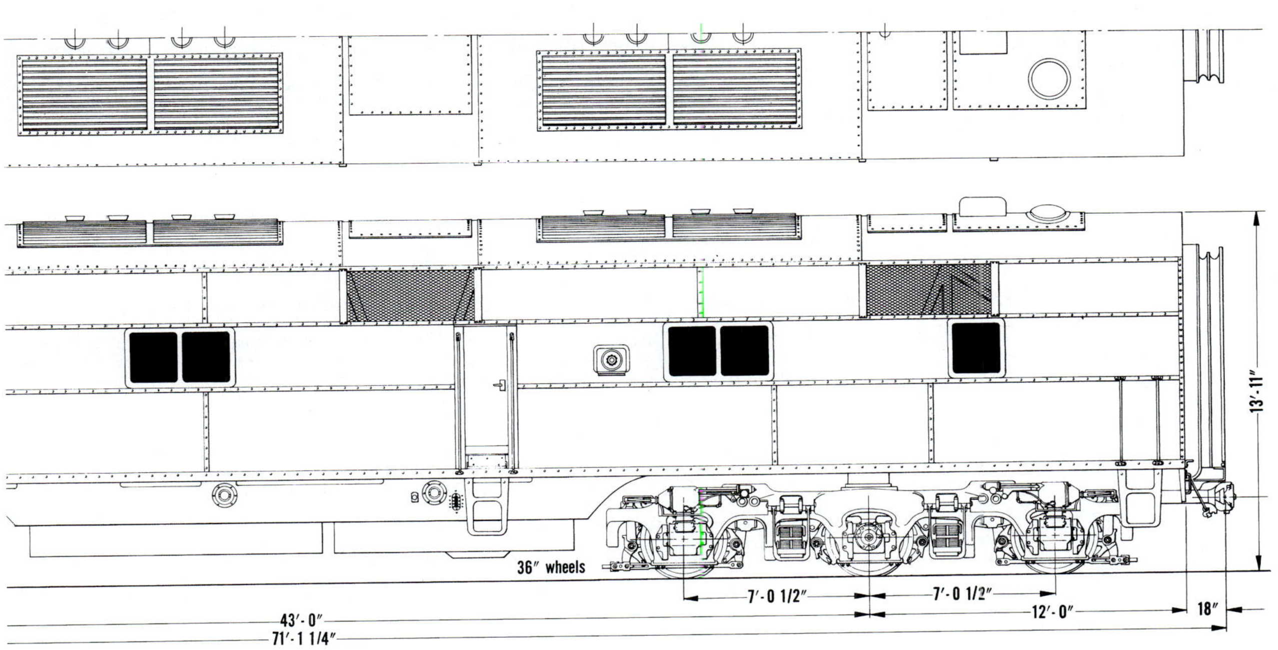

DIESEL VS. STEAM TESTS AND OBSERVATIONS

E7 vs. Niagara 4-8-4

The definitive published diesel vs. steam test occurred during the month of October 1946 when Paul W. Kiefer, chief engineer of motive power and rolling stock of the New York Central, pitted two 4,000-hp E7 sets against six Niagara 4-8-4s* in premium passenger service between Harmon, N. Y., and Chicago, 928 miles. Kiefer, revered among steam enthusiasts for having designed not only the Niagara but the Hudson (4-6-4) before it, wrote about the contest in a thin, red-bound tome titled *A Practical Evaluation of Railroad Motive Power* (Steam Locomotive Research Institute Inc., 1947).

Selectively read, the book heartened traditionalists. Each E7 duo averaged 28,954 miles in October, barely shading the average 4-8-4 production of 27,221. Average annual operating costs per mile, including everything from depreciation and insurance to the crews' vacation time and social security taxes, was computed at $1.22 for the 4-8-4, $1.11 for the two-unit E7. In one area there was no contest. The 4,000-hp E7 required more than twice the time and nearly three times the distance to move a 15-car, 1,005-ton train from zero to 80 mph; even a 6,000-hp, three-unit E7 couldn't equal the 6,600-hp Niagara. But Kiefer had to admit that one month didn't equal a year, that in winter steam was subject to loss of pressure, frozen ash pans, semi-frozen coal, and intermediate refueling.

In effect, the conclusion of the tests appeared on the cover of the February 15, 1947, *Railway Age*, in a color Electro-Motive ad headlined, "The *Century* Passes Its Millionth Mile Behind General Motors Diesel Power." In those days, where the *Century* went, the Central followed.—*David P. Morgan*

(Excerpted from TRAINS *magazine editor David P. Morgan's article "The Essence of the E7," which appeared in the January 1979 issue of* TRAINS.*)*

* The New York Central bought 26 class S-1a and S-1b 4-8-4 Niagaras from Alco in 1945-1946. They were retired in 1956.

Another summary of the battle of steam and diesel comes from J.W. Hawthorne, who served as Central of Georgia's Superintendent of Motive Power in 1945 when the railroad—all-steam except for a group of diesel switchers—received its first road diesels, a group of passenger E7s. "Whereas under steam-engine conditions we could rarely reach 100,000 miles between engine failures, diesel locomotives achieved five times this mileage as a commonplace record. In addition, delays formerly occurring daily for coaling and watering steam locomotives, lubricating rods, cleaning ashpans, and other regular—and time-consuming—maintenance vanished from our 8 a.m. operations report."

the nose: gone was the long, 70-degree slanted nose of early Es; in its place was the same 80-degree "bulldog" nose of the FT. Although many feel this took away from the sleek aesthetics and look of speed of the early Es, to EMD this simplified production. The shorter nose was easier and less expensive to produce, resulted in more interior space, and having the same nose on Es and Fs made sense. The bulldog nose also allowed conventional nose doors, something only an expensive variation allowed on early Es (with the E4).

The sides and roof remained largely the same as the E6, with rectangular screen-covered air intakes, rectangular side windows, and louvers covering the radiator fans on the roof.

With such a large number of E7s built, and the production spanning four years, a number of details and spotting features (as well as buyer options) varied throughout production. Multiple types of air horns and headlights were a buyer option. Most opted for a pair of single-note horns, one pointing in each direction, but some railroads opted

Union Pacific acquired 13 E7s (six A units) in August 1946, including E7A 959A and E7B 961B. The A unit has the screen-type access door behind the cab door, and a cast pilot as found on earlier UP E units. The 959A was renumbered 998 in 1948. *Union Pacific*

Chicago & Eastern Illinois E7 1101 leads the Louisville & Nashville's *Georgian* southbound at Englewood Station in Chicago in August 1949. The railroad had three E7s to handle its own passenger trains as well as those of L&N, for which it served as its Chicago connection. *Bob Milner*

for multi-chime horns (from Nathan or Leslie).

An option on a majority of E7s (and later Es) was a lower headlight mounted on the nose door. Headlights (upper and lower) varied in style by railroad. Some used the upper as the main headlight and some the lower, with the other headlight as a signal light or Mars (moving) light.

Another nose-related option was the number board. Most E7s were equipped with small housings including the number board and—at the front end of the board—a classification light on each side of the nose just below the level of the headlight. Several railroads, however, opted for larger number boxes mounted at a 45-degree angle on the nose, with the class lamp centered above it on the nose.

The pilot style was another buyer option. Most received the so-called "passenger" pilot, a rounded, smooth style that included a cover for a retractable (hydraulically operated) coupler. Some railroads opted for E7s with the "freight" pilot—the design that was the standard on F units—which had a

Wabash owned four E7As including no. 1000, which was built in August 1946. The gray, blue, and white locomotive has a full-width diaphragm at the rear.
Electro-Motive Division

This roof view of an E7 under construction shows the rear end with conventional diaphragm; roof hatch with steam generator exhaust and vent; and four exhaust stacks for each engine, straddled by louvered covers for radiator fans. The small filler to the left of each radiator panel are for cooling (radiator) water.
Electro-Motive Division

notched recess below the anticlimber and an opening for a non-retractable coupler (as on the Boston & Maine E7 on page 96).

All E7s were equipped with MU (multiple-unit) connections. This includes multiple air hoses on either side of the coupler that connect various air brake functions among locomotives, as well as a socket for connecting a multi-pin-connector electrical cable to relay engine and other commands among MU-ed locomotives.

As built, many E7As had MU connections only at the rear, with the thought that an A unit would either lead or trail the locomotive consist. Railroads soon discovered that operating flexibility outweighed aesthetics, and began operating A units nose-to-tail with other A units or within groups of three or more locomotives. The result was that MU connections

Southern Pacific's red and orange *Daylight* scheme would eventually be adopted for all of its E units. Here E7 6003A and two B units are lettered for the *Shasta Daylight,* including a separate nose medallion. The engine was built in August 1947.
Electro-Motive Division

became standard at the front of A units (and were often added later to older E units).

For A units, locomotives with MU connections usually have a small hinged hatch located on the nose next to the headlight (sometimes a hatch on both sides) covering the socket for the MU cable. Locomotives also had multiple air hose connections below the anticlimber on either side of the coupler, along with a steam line connector and the train line air brake and signal hoses.

Several side opening and side access door details changed during E7 production. There's a small vertical access panel on each side, immediately behind the cab door. On early E7s these doors had horizontal louvers running down their height. Mid-production locomotives have plain panels, and late-production E7s have panels with upper and

Bangor & Aroostook E7 no. 11 pauses at Caribou, Maine, in May 1960. The railroad had two E7s, originally numbered 700-701 and later renumbered 10-11.
J. David Ingles collection

The screened air-intake openings and abbreviated side windows mark Boston & Maine no. 3820 as a late E7A. It was built in April 1949; the railroad had 21 E7s (all A units) built from 1946 to 1949.
Electro-Motive Division

lower openings covered by fine-screen-mesh.

The sides on most E7s followed a standard pattern. The upper sides have three rectangular air-intake openings, covered by screen wire (sometimes called "chicken wire," although it was more substantial—more like chain link), with parts of the side truss framework visible behind the screen. Just below that, there are three windows: two two-panel rectangular openings, with a square single-panel window toward the rear.

On late E7s, there's an additional air intake panel at the upper rear. These also have only two windows—both square—with a series of six staggered screened engine-air-intake panels added across the middle (see the New York Central locomotive above).

For all of these details, it's important to remember that many railroads received multiple orders of E7s spanning several years, and they remained in service long enough that many were modified during their service lives. This means all E7s of a

New York Central E7 no. 4023 leads a train at South Bend, Ind., in April 1962. The NYC had 36 E7As (nos. 4000-4036) and 14 B units (4100-4113). Number 4023, built in April 1947, has modified side windows and added air-intake openings. *J. David Ingles collection*

A Pennsylvania E7 leads a commuter train on the New York & Long Branch in April 1956. Number 5879, built in April 1949, has nose lift rings and unique-to-the-PRR separate number boxes and a rooftop Trainphone antenna. Pennsy had more E7s than any other railroad (46 As, 14 Bs). *Don Wood*

given railroad may vary in individual details. If you're modeling, check a photo of a specific locomotive at a specific time to be sure the details match.

The era of custom-equipped locomotives had largely passed by the end of the war, but there were a few railroad-specific variations among E7s. The E7s assigned to the joint St. Louis-San Francisco and Missouri-Kansas-Texas *Texas Special* had corrugated stainless steel panels along the lower sides. The Frisco would later modify the sides of its E7s to match E8s, including four portholes and a stainless-steel grille along the length of each side.

The Burlington, famous for the stainless-steel fluted sides on its E5s and earlier power cars, outfitted many E7s (and later E units) with stainless-steel side panels. And Missouri Pacific's E7s were delivered with portholes instead of rectangular windows, also to match its earlier E units.

The E7 was a resounding success, with 28 railroads ordering them new, with several

Missouri Pacific ordered its E7s with round portholes. Number 7010 and a B unit are on a train at St. Louis Union Station.
Missouri Pacific

At first glance, St. Louis-San Francisco no. 2004 looks like an E8. However, it's an E7—the railroad added a stainless grille and four side portholes to match later E units. Wearing gold-leaf paint striping, the 2004 and an E8 in Dulux Gold striping lead the *Will Rogers* at Webster Groves, Mo., in December 1960. Frisco named its E units after famous horses.
J. David Ingles collection

additional railroads eventually owning them through mergers. With some of the first E7s, railroads were still assigning locomotives to specific trains; by the late 1940s, most railroads had enough of them that they operated them in general passenger pools where any locomotive could cover any train. Gone were most of the train-specific lettering schemes and the custom body stylings and modifications of early Es.

The E7 largely accomplished the task of bumping steam locomotives from major passenger trains. Longtime *Trains* magazine editor David P. Morgan noted that the E7, during its four-year production run, was largely responsible for increasing the diesel locomotive's share of passenger-train car-miles pulled from 9.6 percent in 1945 to 49.3 percent in 1949.

Railroads were still testing locomotives to make sure they weren't making a mistake with the newfangled technology (see "Diesel vs. Steam" on page 92). Even railroads that ordered or built passenger steam locomotives after the war (such as New York Central and Pennsylvania) wound up with E7s, and the Pennsy, for example, found its initial pair of E7s (delivered in September 1945) racking up several times the mileage that any of its new

Original-scheme Florida East Coast E7 no. 1008 is looking a bit worse for wear as it and another E7 in the newer blue scheme lead a train at West Palm Beach, Fla., in May 1961. The FEC owned 17 E7As and 3 E7Bs.
J. David Ingles collection

trouble-prone T1 4-4-4-4 steam locomotives could produce.

As good as it was, the E7 was, of course, not perfect. It excelled in sustained high-speed flatland running. Railroads that tried running them in the mountains on long, steep grades often reconsidered—Great Northern kept its on level territory, opting for Fs on its transcontinental trains, as did Santa Fe (which had its early Es rebuilt but never ordered later E units). Rio Grande, Northern Pacific, and Western Pacific never owned an E, opting for steam-generator-equipped Fs on their grades; railroads with slower-paced trains also opted for Fs, including Chicago Great Western and Soo Line. Others had large groups of both Es and Fs in passenger service, including Southern, Chicago & North Western, and Southern Pacific.

As the 1940s were drawing to a close, locomotives continued to evolve and

Milwaukee Road E7 no. 17B is at Madison, Wis., wearing its as-delivered *Hiawatha* scheme. The small angled number boards were unique to the Milwaukee (the factory boards are painted over). The railroad owned 10 E7As, built in May and June 1946.
Trains magazine collection

Louisville & Nashville E7 791 and E6 754 lead the *Georgian* into St. Louis Union Station in December 1965. Both locomotives have been modified with air-intake openings in the middle side panels; the E7 has new headlights and an external nose MU socket. *J. David Ingles*

The Rock Island owned 11 E7As and 9 E7Bs. Number 632, built in April 1946, is at Peoria, Ill., in June 1957. *J. David Ingles collection*

improve, and the competition—although still not significant—had also improved. Alco's PA, with a reputation for handling tough grades that the E could not, was the biggest challenger. It was time again for EMD to revamp its locomotive line, and its passenger diesel would receive a major upgrade.

Of one thing there was no doubt—dieselization was well on its way. Despite the pleas of steam builder Lima (which built its last steam locomotive in 1949) and steam stalwarts Norfolk & Western (which built the last of its J-class 4-8-4 passenger locomotives in 1950) and Illinois Central (which had at least invested in passenger diesels, but not freight), it would be less than a decade before steam was all but gone from U.S. rails. For passenger service, it would be the new E8 that would be largely responsible for finishing the job.

LOCOMOTIVE GRILLES

Long stainless-steel grilles were used to cover the top openings on the sides of E8s and E9s as well as late F3s, F7s, and F9s. These are a spotting feature, as they came in two basic types. The first ones on E8s and late (Phase IV) F3s were fabricated, with horizontal slats fixed to vertical posts. Two intermediate heavy horizontal pieces divided the grille into thirds. The panels came in different lengths to fit various locomotive models.

Starting in late 1951 (late in F7 and E8 production) these were changed to a stamped design, with three horizontal rows of vertical slits or louvers. These were Far-Air Dynamic Grilles, made by the Farr Company (and yes, the spelling was different between the company name and the trademarked product; the company sold other filter products as well). They were less expensive, and Farr's advertising and promotional materials touted them as acting like inertial filters, with the louver design creating air flow that kept particulates from entering the openings when the locomotive was moving.

Early stainless-steel grilles were fabricated, with horizontal slats (five per section) secured to vertical members. They were applied in sections, with double vertical posts (at left) marking section divisions. *Two photos: Electro-Motive Division*

Far-Air grilles (made by the Farr Co.) featured stamped vertical louvers in three horizontal rows. They began appearing on E and F units in late 1951, and were sometimes applied to older locomotives as well.

As built in 1947, St. Louis-San Francisco E7 2002 had stainless-steel fluted lower sides for service on the *Meteor* (as did E7s 2001, 2004, and 2005). Sister E7s 2000 and 2003 also had fluting but carried lettering for the joint SLSF/ Missouri-Kansas-Texas *Texas Special*. They ran this way through 1950. *St. Louis-San Francisco*

The E8 represented a major mechanical and performance upgrade compared to the E7, with a horsepower boost to 2,250, improved traction motors, and the option of dynamic brakes. Demonstrator no. 952 emerged from LaGrange in April 1949 (EMD's test car is behind it).
Electro-Motive Division

In 1949, General Motors built a large (2" = 1 foot) cutaway model of an E8 to highlight its construction. It nicely illustrates how the truss sides are built and how the various components fit inside the body.

Trains magazine collection

Chesapeake & Ohio E7 4513 (former Pere Marquette) and E8 4013 (built in November 1951) await departure from Detroit in August 1962.

J. David Ingles

Roof construction on the E8 featured the same modular fans as on F7s. The boxy housings are winterization hatches. This locomotive has two steam generators (two stacks and two vents on the near hatch). *Electro-Motive Division*

Major upgrade: the E8

The E8, introduced in August 1949 (demonstrator no. 952 emerged in April 1949), represented a major upgrade to EMD's E unit line. The E8 was introduced to replace the E7 at the same time the company brought out the freight-service F7 to replace the F3.

Mechanically the E8 was still a twin-engine, A1A-A1A diesel locomotive. The engines were the upgraded 12-cylinder 567B, which featured a simplified lube oil system and other improvements. The biggest internal change was the new D15A generator and D27B traction motors, which bumped the horsepower to 2,250. The

ELECTRO-MOTIVE DIVISION E8A

Above middle: Two former Erie E8s back onto Train 6, the *Lake Cities*, at Dearborn Station in Chicago on June 25, 1961. They're still wearing the Erie scheme but are lettered Erie-Lackawanna for the railroad's just-completed merger with Delaware, Lackawanna & Western. *J. David Ingles*

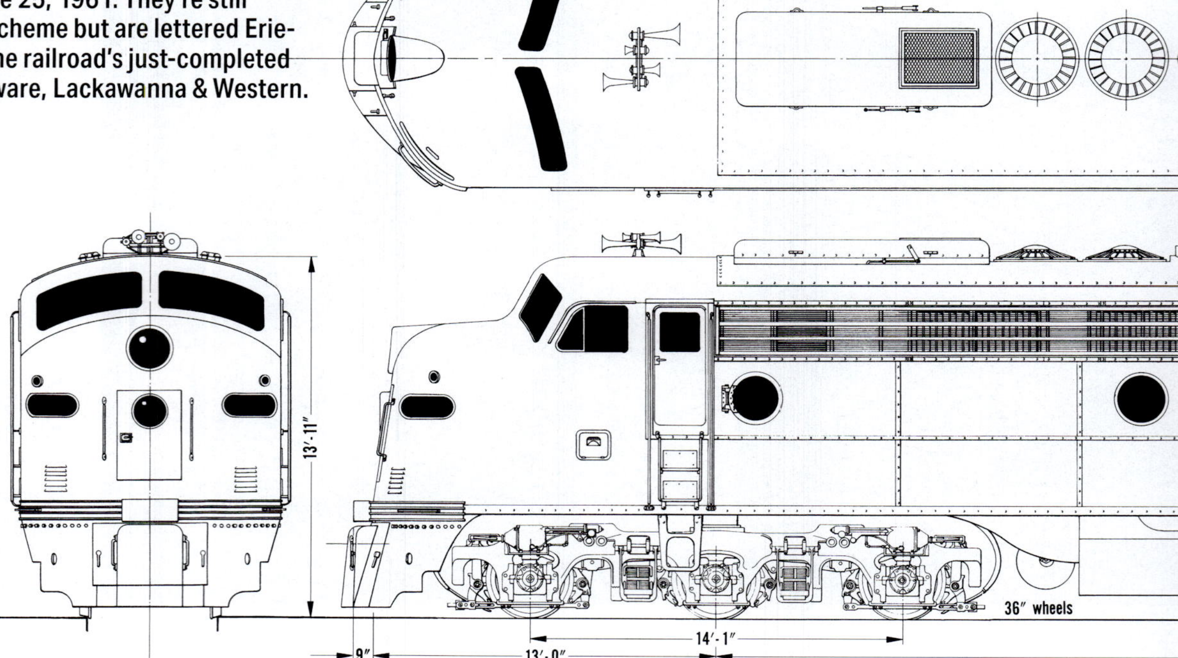

New York Central E8 no. 4050 (in the "cigar band" scheme) and a pair of E7s lead train no. 3 at Elkhart, Ind., on July 21, 1965. The railroad acquired 60 E8s, all A units, from 1951-1953.
J. David Ingles

upgraded electrical equipment also gave the locomotives better acceleration and allowed an 825-amp continuous load—more than earlier motors—and improved the short-time load above that by 40 percent under maximum amperage load, making them more suitable on grades or heavy trains compared to E7 and earlier units.

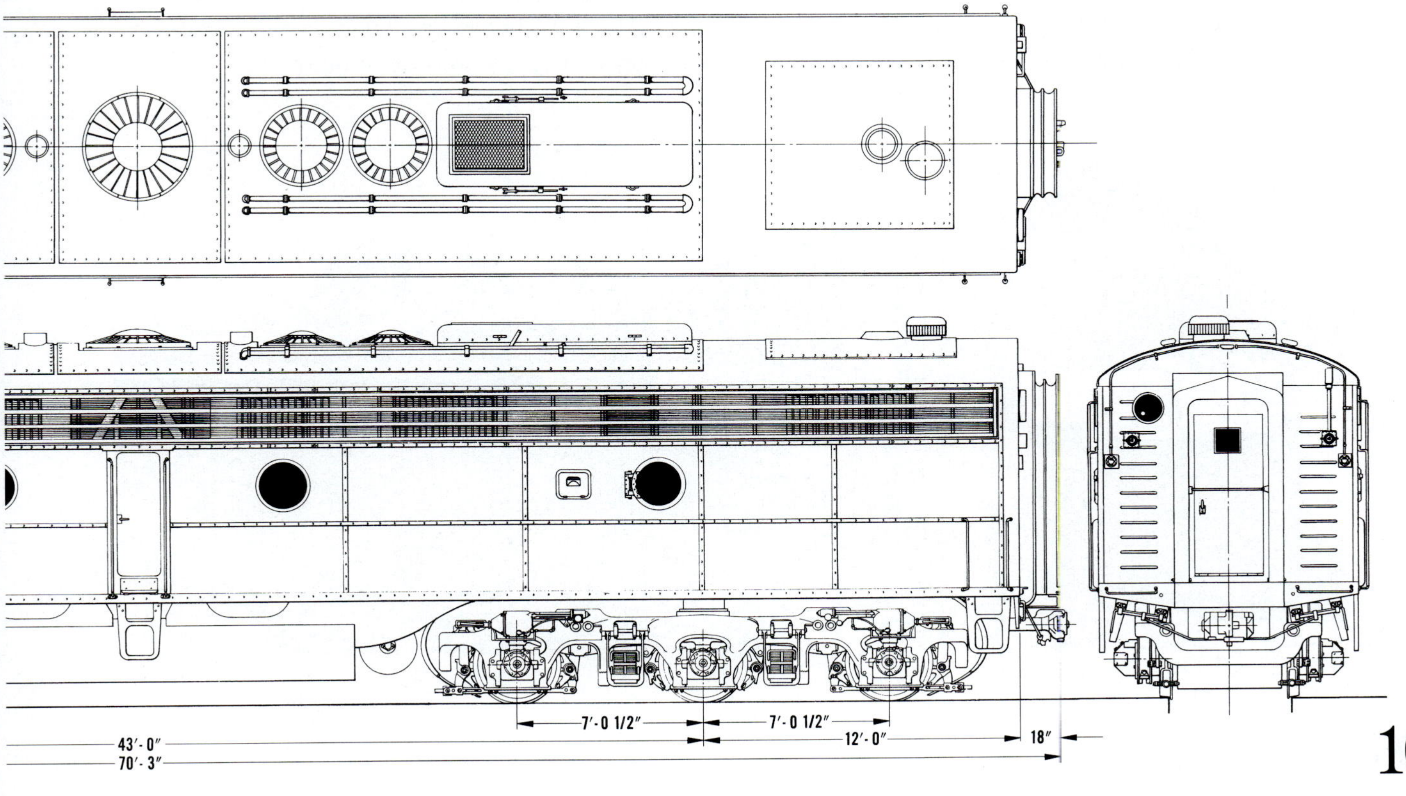

Inside, the locomotive was revamped. The engine orientation was changed so that the engines faced each other, with the generators on the outboard ends (to the front and back). This placed the generators closer to their trucks and shortened high-voltage cable runs. Wiring, piping, and engine ancillary equipment were redesigned and moved to racks, and the wiring cabinets were relocated. Modular components were used whenever possible to replace individual hard-wired components, shortening assembly time and making maintenance easier.

The E8 was the first EMD passenger diesel available with dynamic braking. On locomotives so equipped, the hatch at the center of the locomotive roof between the engines had the same modular housing (roof

TRAIN OF TOMORROW

The growth of diesel passenger service through the 1940s was reflected by a number of publicity events, many staged by railroads to inaugurate new trains or equipment or by builders introducing new products and new technology. Among the best known and most dramatic was General Motors' *Train of Tomorrow*, a four-car set of dome-equipped passenger cars pulled by a new E7 diesel. Launched in 1947, the train logged more than 65,000 miles while stopping for public exhibition events in 182 cities through October 1949. More than 5.7 million people toured the train on these stops, and it was seen in operation by millions more.

The four cars were built by Pullman-Standard: a coach, diner, sleeper, and observation car, all equipped with what P-S called Astra-Domes and built of low-alloy, high-tensile steel and Thermopane glass. The locomotive was an E7 (no. 765) in a blue-gray scheme with fluted siding and a shooting star logo and "Train of Tomorrow" lettering on each side. Following the end of the tour, the entire train was sold to Union Pacific (the E7 was re-numbered UP 988).

The genesis of the *Train of Tomorrow* is credited to EMD general manager Cyrus Osborn, who noted while riding an F unit in the Rocky Mountains that "a lot of people would pay $500 for this fireman's seat if they could see from it." Thus was hatched the idea of the dome car, with windows above and forward allowing much better views of surrounding scenery than a standard passenger-car window.

The project started with a 45-foot-long scale model of the train—which cost $101,772—displayed in suburban Chicago. Invitations to view the display went to officials from more than 50 railroads, with the goal to promote diesel-powered passenger trains and show railroads and car builders how to spur interest in rail travel.

All major car builders did indeed introduce dome cars of various designs in their streamlined trains through the 1950s, and it became a common marketing tool to emphasize that trains were dome equipped.

hatch, grid, and fan) as on the F7. Dynamic brakes are not as critical for passenger trains as freight, but some railroads—especially those operating in areas with significant grades—wanted it as an option. Railroads opting for dynamics on their E8s included Milwaukee Road, Southern (on 10 of 17), Southern Pacific, and Union Pacific.

Visually the E8 was significantly different compared to earlier Es. Although the body itself was still built with the same frame and side truss assemblies, the truss arrangement was altered both to accommodate the new engine/generator arrangement and to simplify final assembly with subassemblies.

Gone were the upper rectangular screened openings, replaced by openings covered by a stainless-steel grille that ran the length of the side from behind the cab door to the rear. These were initially fabricated, with horizontal slats attached to a series of vertical posts, and applied as several panels. Toward the end of production (after September 1951), these were replaced by stamped Far-Air grilles (technically Far-Air Dynamic Grilles, made by the Farr Co.; see page 101) These can be spotted by their three horizontal rows of vertical slits. They were more economical than the earlier fabricated grilles, and the Farr Co. marketed them as being passive filters as well, creating air flow that kept foreign particles from getting through the grille openings.

Instead of rectangular windows—which were prone to leaking on older Es—the middle side panels of the E8 had a series of

Pennsylvania E8 no. 5712 and an E7 are at Kalamazoo, Mich., in October 1960. The locomotive is still in the five-stripe Tuscan scheme, with the Trainphone antenna on the roof. Pennsylvania was the largest E8 owner with 74 A units.
J. David Ingles

The Southern Railway owned 17 E8s, all A units. Number 2928, built in September 1951, nicely shows the early fabricated stainless-steel grille, with horizontal slats over vertical members.
Electro-Motive Division

Two Burlington Route E8s, led by no. 9946A, lead the detouring *North Coast Limited* on the Milwaukee Road at Milwaukee in 1967. The Northern Pacific train usually traveled between the Twin Cities and Chicago via Burlington rails. *Tom Hoffman*

Central of Georgia's entire E8 roster—nos. 811 and 812—lead the Chicago-to-Columbus, Ga., *Seminole* in April 1954. *J. Parker Lamb*

In the 1950s Electro-Motive began promoting its rebuilding program, where trucks, engines, and other components were remanufactured. Number 81 is one of eight E8Am locomotives EMD rebuilt from Santa Fe E1s in 1952 and 1953. The locomotives look like stock E8s, but have a lower horsepower rating (2,000). The engine is on Train 190 at Denver Union Station in September 1967. *Tom Hoffman*

four widely spaced round porthole windows: two sealed and two that could be opened.

The roof had a completely new look, featuring the same style of standard modular radiator fan hatch assemblies found on F7s. Four fans were centered along the roof above each engine. These fans were now electrically powered by an auxiliary alternator coupled to the main generator (and thermostatically controlled), a major upgrade to the belt/shaft-driven fans of E7 and earlier engines. Exhaust stacks were located inboard of the radiator fans.

Winterization hatches above the forward and aft fans were standard. Shutters atop the hatches are open in normal conditions so hot air from radiators is expelled upward; the shutters can be closed in freezing conditions, which re-routes warm air from the radiators back into the engine compartment.

The engines were placed farther forward on the frame, with a wall behind them to create a separate compartment for the steam generator at the rear. This, and more compact routing of cables and piping as well as relocating other components, provided more room at the rear, offering the option to have a pair of steam generators instead of a single unit (they were still available in several capacities). Having two steam generators allowed some redundancy in case of the failure of one unit, which could be problematic especially when an A unit was operating by itself.

A related modification was moving the water tank (steam-generator supply) under the frame, in a combined enclosure with the fuel tank. The 1,200-gallon fuel tank, with a broad U-shaped cross section, is surrounded by the water tank, which has external vertical sides curved at the bottom. The water supply was heated with a steam line, which also served to warm the fuel. This minimized problems with the fuel waxing in cold weather, which can clog filters, and the tank design also provided a

E7, E8, E9 PRODUCTION

Railroad	E7A	E7B	E8A	E8B	E9A	E9B
Alton	7	0	0	0	0	0
ACL	20	10	7	0	0	0
ATSF	0	0	8*	5*	0	0
B&O	18	0	21*	22*	4	0
BAR	2	0	0	0	0	0
B&M	21	0	1	0	0	0
CofG	10	0	2	0	0	0
C&O	4	0	31	0	0	0
C&EI	3	0	0	0	1**	0
C&NW	26	0	21	0	0	0
CB&Q	44	0	40	0	16	0
CP	0	0	3	0	0	0
CRI&P	11	9	14*	0	0	0
DL&W	0	0	11	0	0	0
Erie	0	0	14	0	0	0
FEC	17	3	0	0	5	0
GM&O	0	0	1*	0	0	0
GN	13	0	0	0	0	0
IC	14	4	16	2	10	4
KCS	0	0	5	0	1**	0
L&N	12	0	4	0	0	0
MEC	7	0	0	0	0	0
MILW	10	0	0	0	18	6
MKT	2	0	9	0	0	0
MP	14	8	4	0	0	0
NYC	36	14	62	0	0	0
PRR	46	14	74	0	0	0
PM	8	0	0	0	0	0
RF&P	0	0	15	5	0	0
SLSF	6	0	17	0	0	0
SAL	32	3	11	0	1	0
SLSF	0	0	17	0	0	0
SP&S	1	0	0	0	0	0
SOU	18	0	17	0	0	0
SP	5	10	1	0	9	0
T&P	10	0	8	0	0	0
UP	7	11	18	28	35	34
Wabash	4	0	14	0	0	0

Only original owners shown.
* E8ms: ATSF 8 A, 5 B; B&O 5 A, 6 B; CRI&P 1 A; GM&O 1 A. ** E9ms

Two Baltimore & Ohio E8s—1451 and 1434—lead a train heavy with mail and express in June 1966. The B&O opted for large number boxes, single headlights, and multi-chime horns, and the locomotives are wearing the railroad's late solid-blue scheme. *Craig Willett*

Rock Island E8 no. 654 leads Train 3, the ***Golden State***, at Bureau, Ill., in late 1965. Built in March 1952, the E has been modified with plain side panels (replacing the original portholes) and the addition of an external MU socket on the nose, along with nose and above-window grab irons. *Craig Willett*

Richmond, Fredericksburg & Potomac had a fleet of 15 E8As and 5 E8Bs to handle its passenger traffic, which included trains of Atlantic Coast Line and Seaboard Air Line between Richmond, Va., and Washington, D.C. Number 1001 is an early E8, part of an order of five A-B sets delivered in November and December 1949.

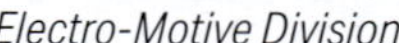
Electro-Motive Division

Differences between E9s and late E8s are minor. Southern Pacific E9A no. 6051 shows the flush headlight lens and Far-Air stamped grille found on all E9s. Number 6051 is one of nine built for SP in December 1954 (nos. 6046-6054).
Electro-Motive Division

Baltimore & Ohio E9 no. 1455 (with an F3B) still wears its original blue, gray, and black scheme at Detroit in July 1963. The railroad owned four E9As (nos. 1454-1457), delivered in May 1955.
J. David Ingles collection

layer of protection for the fuel tank in case of a crash.

Another related change was the trucks. Because E units were becoming heavier, the truck design was modified during E8 production. It's a subtle difference, but the truck frames became heavier, with a deeper (taller) frame. This is most noticeable in looking at the frame near the center axle.

On the nose, the illuminated number board was now larger, but instead of protruding (like the box-style boards on an F7), it was flush with the nose and wrapped around to follow the nose curve, at a level below the upper headlight.

Unlike the E7, EMD did roll out a demonstrator (no. 952) to give railroads a chance to see firsthand the numerous upgrades and improvements to the locomotive.

By the early 1950s, the first E units had been in service for more than a decade, and many had run a million miles or more. With the advances in technology and performance since the late 1930s, EMD promoted a rebuilding and trade-in program for older E units. A railroad could send in an older E and have it rebuilt, re-using many

Above: A pair of Chicago, Burlington & Quincy E9s and three E8s lead the combined ***Empire Builder*** and ***North Coast Limited*** past Tower A2 at Western Avenue in Chicago in 1967. The CB&Q used stainless-steel side panels on many of its E units to better match its ***Zephyr*** passenger equipment.
J. David Ingles

Above right: Illinois Central's southbound ***City of New Orleans*** pauses at Homewood, Ill., in July 1965. Leading is E9 no. 4042, built in December 1957. It's one of 10 E9As (nos. 4034-4043) and four E9Bs (4106-4109) bought new by IC; the railroad later bought five used E9As from Florida East Coast.
J. David Ingles

key components that could be refurbished, such as the trucks/wheels, engines, and generators. The result was a locomotive that was essentially new, but at a price lower than a brand-new locomotive.

During E8 production, EMD turned out a total of 26 of these rebuilds, designated E8m, for Santa Fe (13), Baltimore & Ohio (11), Rock Island (1), and Gulf, Mobile & Ohio (1). The resulting locomotives looked just like an E8; the only operational difference was a lower horsepower rating (2,000) because of the re-used electrical equipment.

The E8 proved to be almost as popular as the E7, with 460 (421 A units, 39 Bs) built through the end of production in January 1954. A total of 28 railroads bought them new; leading owners were Pennsylvania (74 A units) New York Central (62 A units), Union Pacific (18 As, 28 Bs), Baltimore & Ohio (21 As, 22 Bs), and Burlington Route (40 As).

An era ends with the E9

The final iteration of the E unit was the E9, introduced in April 1954. The major difference compared to the E8 was the upgraded 567C engine, along with new (D37) traction motors featuring better insulation and durability, giving the E9 a horsepower bump to 2,400. The new engine was extremely reliable, and continued to improve upon earlier designs. The new traction motor again dramatically increased load ratings, and the traction motors and generator provided faster acceleration compared to earlier Es.

Externally the E9 was identical to the last E8s. The only visual change was a flush-mounted headlight lens (also found on the last E8s built for Illinois Central), compared to the recessed lens of earlier E8s. The Far-Air grille was used on all E9s, and E9s with dynamic brakes used a larger (48"-diameter) fan.

By the time the E9 appeared, the E8 (and other models) had pretty much finished the dieselization of American passenger trains. Along with that, passenger trains had begun a decline: passenger train miles and ridership were beginning to drop in the mid-1950s; people were choosing the automobile and airplanes over railroads for intercity travel.

Railroads found they had enough locomotives to power the number of passenger trains that remained, and were reluctant to invest in new locomotives when passenger revenues were dropping and the

Milwaukee Road E9 no. 32C switches a New York Central baggage car as it gets the *Morning Hiawatha* ready for departure at St. Paul in July 1964. The railroad had 18 E9As and 6 E9Bs.
J. David Ingles

Union Pacific owned almost half of all E9s built: 35 A units and 34 Bs. Number 909 is one of the last E9s built, delivered in August 1961. It's at Kansas City, Mo., in June 1967. It has plates above the winterization hatches, horns located atop the hatches, and a roof-top beacon above the cab.
J. David Ingles collection

future of many long-distance trains was uncertain. As a result, even though the model remained in the EMD catalog for 10 years, only 144 E9s (100 As, 44 Bs) were built for 10 railroads. The largest customer was UP, with 35As and 34 Bs.

Passenger ridership continued its downward trend in the 1960s. By the early 1960s, railroads that wanted passenger power were looking for dual-purpose locomotives that could haul either passenger or freight (and, in most cases, that could just be converted to freight when the inevitable end of passenger service came).

The last E unit—and the last streamlined carbody diesel—to roll out of LaGrange was Union Pacific E9A no. 914, one of a group of three E9s (nos. 912-914) delivered in December 1963 and January 1964. Only four other E9s had been built in the 1960s; no doubt the sight of a bulldog nose on the assembly line at EMD turned heads among observers. With no. 914, the book was closed on production of Electro-Motive's streamlined diesels—the locomotives that vanquished steam.

CHAPTER 5

FREIGHT DIESELIZATION

THE F2 AND F3 ADVANCED THE JOB BEGUN BY THE FT

An A-A pair of F3s lean into a curve as they lead a Minneapolis to Waterloo, Iowa, run-through freight (M&StL/Illinois Central) heavy with refrigerator car traffic in March 1955. White flags and white classification lights indicate the train is an extra. The railroad's six F3s, including no. 348, were built in March 1948.
Bob Milner

As World War II wound down, War Production Board limitations were eased and FT production was booming. However, the FT, as revolutionary and successful as it was, suffered from manufacturing and operational inefficiencies. Electro-Motive knew that an upgrade in the form of a new locomotive model was needed to improve performance, power, and efficiency.

The number of items EMD needed to address would go beyond a simple upgrade. In 1944, while the FT was still in production, the designers at EMD began developing a new locomotive model, taking the things that the FT did well, correcting the things that weren't working out, and incorporating newer technology. The company's experiences with its pre-war E units and switchers that had been piling up mileage and operating hours since the late 1930s also influenced design, as EMD looked for as many ways as possible to utilize common components among multiple locomotive models.

The first A-B-B-A demonstrator set for what would become the F3 emerged from the factory in July 1945 as no. 291. (Another demonstrator, no. 754, with high-speed gearing and steam generators, toured in 1946—it was an A-B-A set, using one of the Bs from the original demonstrator.) The plan was to introduce the new locomotive model at the same time as the new E7 passenger diesel. However, issues with the F's new main generator (Es and Fs used different generator models because of their different engine sizes) led to a delay in production; what was to have been the F2 was delayed and renamed the F3, and a short-term interim model, the F2, bridged the gap.

Redesign and the F2

A key in designing the new locomotive was an expansion of the building-block principle, so that the new model's design

Electro-Motive F3 demonstrator no. 291 emerged in July 1945, but problems with the new generator delayed F3 production locomotives until November 1946. Early F3s were marked by three evenly spaced portholes. *Electro-Motive Division*

The F2 was an intermediate model built briefly until the new D12 generator was ready for production. It represented a radical departure in construction and appearance from the FT, and was identical externally to the first F3s. Boston & Maine no. 4260 was built in July 1946.
Electro-Motive Division

The Burlington Route nose herald would be applied by the railroad, so the space is blank on the builder's photo of no. 153A. The Burlington received 10 F2As in July 1946 to match its earlier FT A-B sets to create three-unit consists.
Electro-Motive Division

Rock Island bought 12 red and black F2As in July 1946. Its goal was also to divide its four-unit FTs into A-B sets and pair each set with an F2 to create a three-unit diesel.
Electro-Motive Division

TRACTION-MOTOR TRANSITION AND LOADING

With the direct-current traction motors on early diesels, it was critical to not overload them beyond their rated amperage limits. With heavy trains and/or steep grades—especially when starting—traction motors can easily draw higher-than-rated amperage, which can cause overheating and failure of components.

Traction motors all had a sustained amperage level at which they could operate safely without damage (the continuous motor rating) and a time period at which they could temporarily operate (short-time rating) above this rating. A key in running the locomotive is the ammeter, which shows how much current is being used. The meter shows the continuous rating in green, with short-time ratings in yellow and red at right (the higher the amperage, the shorter the time the needle can remain there). The graphic at right shows an ammeter from an F3; note that any amperage above 700 is a short-time rating, with numbers indicating how far the locomotive can run at each amperage level.

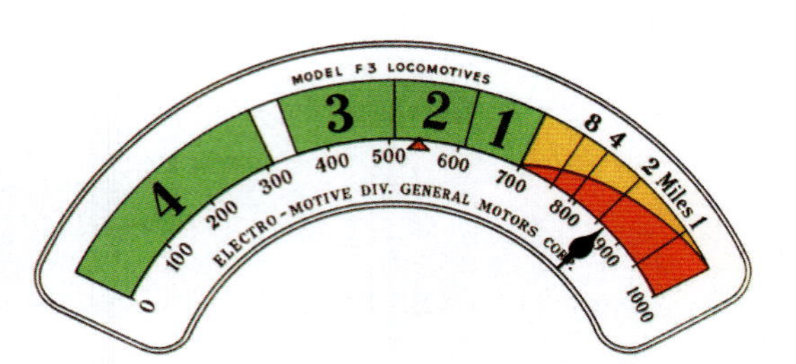

The ammeter indicates how many amperes are being drawn by the traction motors. The numbers in green show the transition steps appropriate for the current; the short-time rating is in red. The needle is shown at just over 850 amps, meaning the engineer can only operate the locomotive in this range for just under 2 miles before damage will occur. *Electro-Motive Division*

Tied to this was the need to make electrical transitions for how current is delivered from the generator to the traction motors. These transitions were numbered 1 to 4, with the transition lever on the left of the throttle control stand. On the ammeter, numbers in the green areas guide the engineer on when to change the settings.

In position 1 (series-parallel), used when starting, the nos. 1 and 4 traction motors are connected electrically in series, as are the nos. 2 and 3 motors; the two sets of motors are then connected in parallel. The motors will draw their highest current when starting.

As speed increases and amperage drops, the transition lever is moved to no. 2 (series-parallel-shunt). This is the same as no. 1, but with the fields of each traction motor shunted by resistors.

As the ammeter drops further, the transition lever is then moved to no. 3 (parallel), which connects all four traction motors in parallel. If speed increases sufficiently again and the ammeter drops to the next level, the transition lever is moved to no. 4 (parallel-shunt), which is the same as 3 but with the traction motor fields shunted by resistors.

If current draw begins to increase (as when starting up a grade), transition is then made backward as far as needed.

Transition was manual on the first FTs, became automatic as an option on F3s, and became automatic as standard on the F9. Many earlier locomotives were later modified with automatic transition.

would reflect the view that each A and B unit were separate locomotives as opposed to an A-B set being a single locomotive. The FT had foreshadowed this, but it would be continued by the new design and further on subsequent F units.

Another key was streamlining manufacturing steps and efficiency. Each FT took about 40,000 man-hours to build; the goal was for the new locomotive to trim that time significantly. To do this, as many components as possible were designed as modules and subassemblies to simplify final assembly.

The result was a new locomotive with a significantly different appearance, as the photo of demonstrator 291 shows (page 116). However, the upgrade was far more than just a spotting feature change of four portholes to three. It represented an extensive redesign of both the A and B carbodies themselves, as well as many of the major components within.

Internally, the new model had an

The first F3s were known as Phase I engines, marked by three side portholes and four tall (shrouded) radiator fans on the roof. Monon had F3s for both freight and passenger service. Here steam-generator-equipped 82B (built in May 1947) leads the *Tippecanoe* at Hammond, Ind., in 1954.

Trains magazine collection

EMD CUSTOMER SERVICE AND SUPPORT

One of the key reasons Electro-Motive was so successful with early diesels as well as newer E and F units through the 1940s and '50s was the company's extensive customer service and support network, and its responsiveness to customers' problems and concerns. Preston Cook outlined many of these processes in a *Railfan & Railroad* article ("Electro-Motive's FT Celebrates 50 Years," October 1989).

Recognizing that railroads at the time had little experience with diesels, EMD trained instructors and service personnel and sent them out with locomotives being delivered. They rode with crews on the locomotives' initial runs and offered classes and extensive training and instruction manuals to aid in maintaining and running the diesels. Electro-Motive also provided broader instructions and advice on setting up shop and parts facilities. A fundamental principle at EMD was allowing lower-level management personnel to quickly find and implement solutions when working with customers. If railroads had problems, they could quickly communicate with someone at EMD to find a fix.

Another key, according to Cook, was EMD's extensive parts departments and repair facilities that were located throughout the country. Railroads rarely had to wait long for warranty or contract repairs or replacement parts.

F3 CUTAWAY DRAWING

1. 16-cylinder 567B engine
2. Main generator
3. Companion alternator
4. Electrical cabinet
5. Traction motors
6. Radiator
7. Lube oil cooler
8. Radiator fans
9. Lube oil filter tank
10. Dynamic brake (optional)
11. Fuel tank
12. Blomberg B truck
13. Steam generator (optional)
14. Air compressor
15. Generator/traction motor blowers

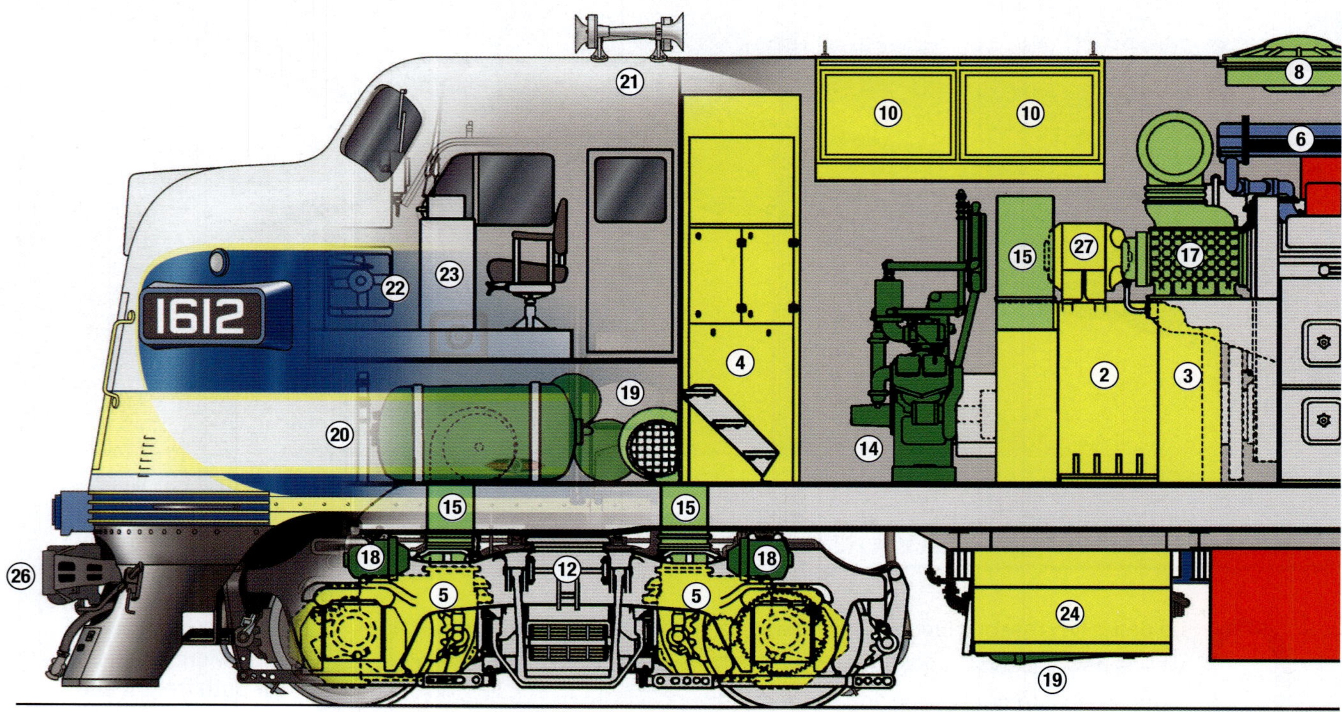

upgraded 16-cylinder 567B engine, which featured improvements to the lube oil system and an aluminum front housing and blower support ducts. This improved reliability, simplified plumbing, and reduced engine weight.

The intention was to match the engine with a new, upgraded main generator—the D12—for a horsepower boost to 1,500. However, problems with the D12 delayed its final approval, so EMD eventually chose to begin building production locomotives with the older D8 generator instead of waiting for the new one, which resulted in the same 1,350-hp rating as the FT. The first F2s were built in July 1946, and only 104 were built before production ended in November 1946. With the D12 ready to go, the first production F3s hit the rails in October 1946.

A source of trouble on the FT was that the radiator cooling fans were operated by a drive mechanism of shafts and belts tied to the engine drive shaft. This required precise

16. Coolant tank
17. Roots blower
18. Brake cylinders
19. Air reservoirs
20. Sand boxes (on side walls)
21. Horns
22. Cab heater
23. Operator's controls
24. Battery compartment
25. Exhaust manifolds
26. Couplers
27. Auxiliary generator
28. Lube oil strainers

Key: Yellow = Electrical; Blue = Cooling; Orange = Lube oil; Red = Fuel/exhaust; Light green = Blowers/fans; Dark green = Brake system

Preston Cook; Kalmbach Media

alignment during installation (resulting in excessive assembly time), took up a lot of space in the engine room, and was a maintenance headache—especially since the FT radiator was divided, so required two fan drives for groups of fans fore and aft of the engine. Adding to the headache was that the fans had to be turned on and off manually as needed, meaning the fireman had to walk back through four moving locomotives and clutch the fans in and out of their drives as operating conditions and outside temperature changed.

The F2 introduced a new fan design, with electrically controlled fans powered by an auxiliary alternator, which was coupled to the shaft near the main generator. The radiator core—now centered above the engine—was cooled by four 36"-diameter fans. The fans were modular in design, and were built into the center roof panel directly above the engine (with two exhaust stacks, one behind the forward fan and one in front of the aft fan). The fans pulled air upward

As a training aid for railroads, EMD sent F units with removable panels on a tour to railroads that were buying or interested in F3s. The truss side construction is apparent. From the rear of the locomotive (at left) is the steam generator, 16-cylinder engine, generator, dynamic brake (under roof panel), electrical cabinet, and water tank (just to the right of the center of the right truck).
Electro-Motive Division

A traction motor rests next to a geared axle in a Louisville & Nashville shop in the 1950s. When installed, the small pinion gear on the traction motor engaged the large axle-mounted gear. Choosing gears with different numbers of teeth enabled the motor to provide more power at low speeds or a higher maximum speed.
William A. Akin

through the radiator; the air was drawn in through the side openings.

The new fans reduced labor in installation, as the roof panels were a drop-in assembly. They eliminated the mechanical drive, which opened space inside the engine room and simplified fan repair and replacement. The fans were now automatically (thermostatically) controlled, greatly reducing the chances of overheating or freezing, making for a more reliable locomotive. The new auxiliary alternator also allowed the traction-motor blowers to be electrically powered instead of mechanically driven from a take-off shaft, which further simplified assembly, freed space, and increased reliability.

Dynamic brakes remained an option on the F2 and F3, and more than 60 percent of them would be so equipped. Moving the radiator allowed the dynamic brake grid to move forward in the locomotive, and with the increased interior space, the grid and fan were both located under—and built into—the forward roof hatch directly behind the cab (no more exterior housing as on the FT). The fans were internal, but the presence of dynamics was marked by a pair of screen-covered rectangular openings running lengthwise to the locomotive on the roof hatch. As with the radiator fans, this design allowed for faster assembly and easier maintenance and replacement.

Internal wiring was redesigned, with shorter wire runs whenever possible. The generator remained on the engine end that faced the front of the locomotive. The electrical cabinet was repositioned to become the cab back wall, with access doors to the engine room on either side (a central door was used on the FT, requiring a pass-through aisle at the front of the engine room). All fluid systems (cooling, oil, fuel) were also revised to limit piping runs and simplify construction and maintenance.

The body and frame were changed, and the body truss design was revised. Truck spacing was extended—it was 27'-3" for

Spokane, Portland & Seattle had three F3s for passenger service, all equipped with steam generators and geared to 59:18 to provide a top speed of 80 mph. Number 800, built in April 1947, is ready to back to its train at Pasco, Wash., in this undated image.
Bill Frasier

Above: Number 1615 is one of three ex-Gulf, Mobile & Ohio F3s repainted for Illinois Central Gulf following the railroads' 1972 merger. The 1615 (ex-GM&O 806A) is a Phase I F3 built in December 1946. It's with an ex-Great Northern F7 and another ex-GM&O F3. *J. David Ingles*

Opposite top: Although Canadian National did eventually purchase F3s, this photo is actually a retouched print of F3 demonstrator 754 with the nose shield airbrushed out and CN lettering added. These had steam generators and 59:18 (80 mph) gearing; they were eventually sold to the Monon. *Canadian National*

the FT A and 26'-6" for the FT B—and standardized at 30'-0" for both A and B units (it would remain that way through the F9). Gone were the multiple lengths of B units as on the FT. The F2A and later A units were longer than the FTA (49'-2" compared to 47'-6"); B units were similar (47'-0" on the F2, 46'-9" on the standard FTB). The stretched truck spacing and centering the trucks eliminated the long rear overhang of the standard FT B unit. The new B unit was made to be mechanically the same as the A (with the exception of the cab), unlike the FTB, which relied on its A unit for batteries, again simplifying assembly.

The rear of the F2 and F3 A unit and both ends of the B unit were modified to make couplers standard instead of drawbars. Railroads could still request drawbars, but they would be fitted to coupler draft-gear openings instead of the other way around. The ends received standard hinged doors

ELECTRO-MOTIVE F3

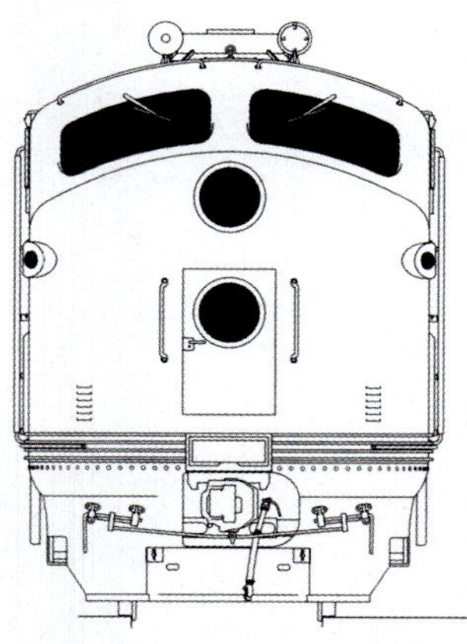

The body details of this drawing reflect a Phase I F3. Although body details, including portholes, side openings, and screens, varied on later versions, the body dimensions remained the same through F3 production. *Kalmbach Media*

754

CANADIAN NATIONAL

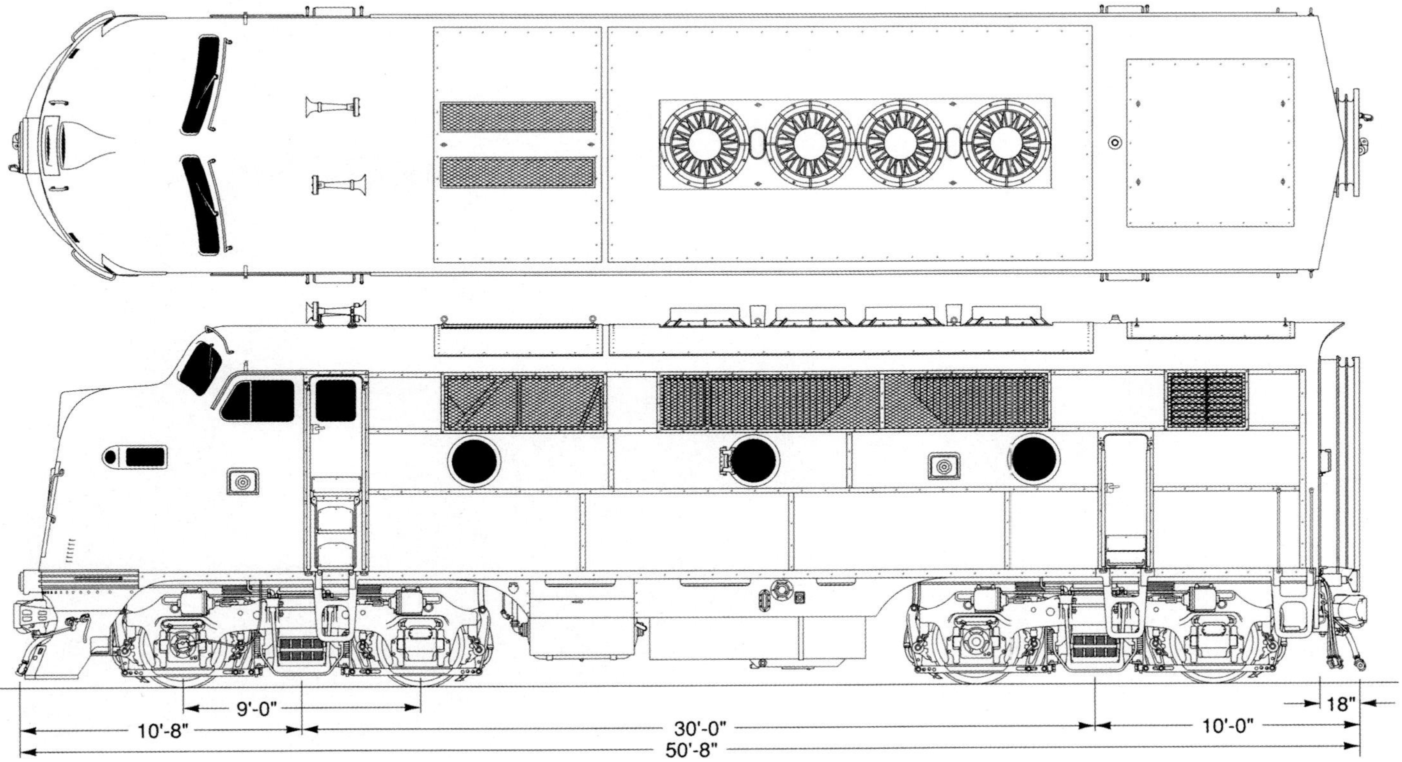

9'-0"

18"

10'-8"

30'-0"

10'-0"

50'-8"

New York Central F3 no. 1618 is at West Detroit, Mich., in 1961. It's an early Phase II F3 built in July 1947, with screen wire between two portholes covering four air intakes, with four tall fans on the roof. *J. David Ingles*

Chicago, Burlington & Quincy Phase IIa F3 set 9962A/B/C leads a southbound freight out of Lincoln, Neb., in November 1961. It's one of three A-B-A sets of former *California Zephyr* passenger locomotives built in October 1947. They were regeared for freight service and had their steam generators removed in 1955. *Jim Seacrest*

Gulf, Mobile & Ohio no. 808B is a Phase IIa F3, built in June 1947. It has a single headlight, large number boxes, no dynamic brakes, a standard ("freight") pilot, and no nose MU. *Electro-Motive Division*

Erie had seven A-B-A sets of F3s for passenger service with steam generators and 58:19 (89 mph) gearing. Phase IIa no. 801 poses with the *Erie Limited* shortly after the locomotive was delivered in July 1947. Erie opted for single headlights and small number boards. *Erie*

Great Northern had F3s for both freight and passenger service. Number 262 is an early Phase II F3 in freight service. It was built in September 1947. *Great Northern*

and diaphragms; ends of mating drawbarred FTs had sliding doors with telescoping frames. Starting with the F2, all bodies had stirrups and vertical grab irons at each end.

The redesigned interior provided more room to add a steam generator and water tank, and many railroads would order F2s, F3s, and later Fs with this equipment. The steam generator itself was located at the rear of either the A or B unit. You can identify engines so equipped by the vent and stack on the rear roof panel.

Space was tight for the steam-generator water supply, so the usual solution was a large tank (1,200 gallons) in the front of the B unit (where the cab would be on an A unit)—see the photo on page 122. Water capacity was more limited on A units, with a maximum of 1,300 gallons in three tanks. However, opting for dynamic brakes

Western Pacific no. 803 is one of three A-B-A sets of passenger-service F3s used on the *California Zephyr*. Shown at West Oakland in April 1948, they were built in June 1947 with 57:20 (95 mph) gearing. They have Phase IIa details, plus dual headlights and large number boxes. *Fred Matthews*

F2 AND F3 PRODUCTION

F2 • July 1946-November 1946			
Railroad	A units	B units	Dates Built
A&EC	2	0	7/46
ACL	12	12	8/46-10/46
B&M	18	3	7/46-10/46
CB&Q	10	0	7/46
CRI&P	12	0	7/46
M&StL	2	1	11/46
NdeM	14	14	8/46-10/46
NYC	2	0	7/46
SOU	2	0	7/46

F3 • October 1946-February 1949			
Railroad	A units	B units	Dates Built
A&R	2	0	4/47, 11/48
A&StAB	1	0	6/47
ACL	12	12	12/48
ATSF	46	46	10/46-1/49
B&O	67	7	7/47-1/49
B&M	2	2	10/48
BAR	9	4	10/47-5/48
C&EI	16	7	2/48-12/48
C&NW	28	11	1/47-12/47
CB&Q	53	52	10/47-1/49
CGW	33	16	10/47-2/49
Clinch	6	3	12/48-2/49
CN	4	2	5/48
CofG	9	0	12/47-5/48
CofNJ	10	5	7/47
D&RGW	6	6	11/46
DL&W	24	16	12/46-3/48
Erie	24	17	11/47-2/49
FEC	8	4	1/49
Georgia	1	0	10/48
GM&O	32	8	12/46-6/47
GN	53	24	11/46-10/48
GTW	22	0	5/48-9/48
KCS	21	20	1/47-10/48
L&N	2	3	8/48
LV	10	10	10/48-11/48

F3 • October 1946-February 1949 (continued)			
Railroad	A units	B units	Dates Built
MILW	8	8	1/49-2/49
MKT	14	7	6/47
Monon	24	6	9/46-4/48 *
MP	64	22	11/47-9/48
NC&StL	9	12	3/48-1/49
NP	25	24	1/47-10/48
NYC	34	18	6/47-4/48
NYO&W	5	2	1/48-3/48
PRR	80	40	7/47-2/49
RDG	6	6	11/48
SAL	11	0	3/48
SLSF	18	18	1/48-6/48
Soo	12	1	10/47-9/48
SOU	102	76	11/46-1/49
SP	80	80	5/47-2/49
SP&S	3	0	4/47-11/48
TP&W	1	1	7/45 **
UP	89	90	9/47-1/49
WM	2	0	6/47
WofA	1	0	9/48
WP	3	6	6/47

* Production locomotives; Monon received former demonstrator F3s built as early as July 1945.
** TP&W's two F3s were former demonstrators built in July 1945
Includes subsidiaries

The F3Bs retained three side portholes throughout production, with screen wire over the upper openings until stainless grilles were added with Phase III locomotives. This Colorado & Southern (Burlington subsidiary) F3B, built in October 1947, has a Phase II body but one of its tall-shrouded fans has been replaced by a new low-profile fan (second from right) by this 1966 photo. *Hol Wagner*

Missouri Pacific F3 no. 525 rests at San Antonio, Texas, in February 1955. The engine, built in November 1947 for subsidiary International-Great Northern, has an early Phase II body with side number boards (painted over), large nose number boxes, and a nose ladder grab and upper-windshield handrails. *William Harry*

eliminated one tank (under the roof hatch behind the cab) and choosing a large steam generator eliminated the option of a small tank located under it.

Beginning with the F2, EMD offered two additional gear ratios: 60:17 (77 mph top speed) and 56:21 (102 mph). This high-speed gearing was chosen notably by Santa Fe for its passenger-equipped F3s and F7s.

A total of 74 F2As and 30 F2Bs were sold through November 1946. The F2s were the first cab units to go south of the border, with 28 (14 As, 14 Bs) to National of Mexico, including four A-B sets with steam generators for passenger service. Many railroads bought F2s to add to FT A-B sets to make them A-B-A consists. Some railroads had found that A-B-B-A FTs provided too much power, and opted to split them into two A-B sets and add an F2 A to each (Boston & Maine, Burlington, Rock Island, and others did this).

The F3

By late 1946, EMD had solved its issues with the D12 generator. It was placed in the

The transition from F3 Phase IIa to Phase IIb was the change to low-profile roof fans, as on Chicago Great Western F3A 111A and F3B 108B, both built in March 1948 and shown at Oelwein, Iowa, in 1965. Both have winterization hatches over the rearmost fan, and the A has added nose grab irons.
C.G. Parsons collection

New Kansas City Southern F3s lead a Chicago Great Western freight eastbound at St. Charles, Ill., in March 1948. The locomotives have the Phase IIb body style.
Henry J. McCord

On F3s with dynamic brakes, the hatch behind the cab has a pair of screen-covered rectangular openings, as on Lehigh Valley no. 518, an F3 built in October 1948. The late Phase II F3 is leading a train at Bethlehem, Pa., in June 1965.
Robert J. Yanosey

new locomotive, which was now rated at 1,500 hp and designated the F3. The only other upgrade compared to the F2 was the addition of an electro-hydraulic governor, an improvement over the electro-pneumatic governor of the FT and F2. It eliminated throttle lag among locomotives being MUed together, allowing instantaneous throttle response among all engines.

The first production F3s, built starting in October 1946, shared the same body as the F2. They can be identified by their three widely spaced side portholes, with screen-covered side openings between the top two horizontal batten strips. Body framework and air-intake louvers are readily visible behind the screen. The four rooftop radiator fans are also quite visible from the side, as

Delaware, Lackawanna & Western F3 no. 661A poses for its builder's photo in March 1948. The DL&W opted for single headlights and a reflectorized front number board on the gray, maroon, and yellow locomotive.
Electro-Motive Division

Bangor & Aroostook was known for its small but long-lived F3 fleet. Number 49, built as 507A in May 1948, is at Northern Maine Junction in September 1978. It has been heavily modified, with winterization hatch (over the rear radiator fan), bell, beacons, fixed lower headlight, and external nose MU connections.
Louis A. Marre collection

Central of Georgia had nine F3As. Number 905, built in May 1948, has a late Phase II body with some extra grab irons, nose MU socket, and pilot footboards. It's at the yard in Savannah, Ga., in April 1959, freshly painted in the railroad's new green and yellow colors. *Central of Georgia*

The Pennsylvania Railroad didn't buy any FTs, but went in big for F3s as it began dieselizing freight operations. The PRR bought 120 F3s (80 A units, 40 Bs) in several orders from July 1947 to February 1949. Phase IIb F3 no. 9518, built in January 1948, shows the Pennsy options of single headlights and small number boards. *Electro-Motive Division*

they have tall shrouds/housings.

The body and interior modifications significantly lessened the assembly time required for new locomotives, and all of the modular and standard components made it much easier to repair, replace, and upgrade parts as the locomotives aged.

The F3 would outsell the FT and become EMD's second-best-selling cab locomotive, with 1,807 built (1,111 A units and 696 B units) for 49 railroads (production numbers vary among sources, usually depending upon whether a few particular locomotives are classified as new or rebuilt). As with the FT, F3s were operated by railroads across the country in all types of service. Production ended in February 1949.

The F3 was chosen in significant numbers specifically for passenger service by several railroads, with 354 equipped with steam generators. Those buying F3s for passenger operations included Santa Fe (42 B units; all paired with A units equipped

The first road freight diesels in Canada were two A-B-A sets of F3s built for Canadian National in May 1948, including no. 9003. Shown here in 1956 at Vancouver, B.C., no. 9003 is a typical Phase IIb engine, still wearing its original green and yellow scheme. *Louis A. Marre collection*

Missouri Pacific no. 576 is a Phase III F3, identifiable by the switch to solid panels between the portholes with louvers covering the engine-air intakes. The upper openings remain covered by screen wire. It's shown shortly after delivery in August 1948. *Missouri Pacific*

Santa Fe passenger F3s 28 and 29 fly green flags as they each lead separate sections of eastbound Train 18, the *Super Chief,* at Albuquerque, N.M., on January 3, 1964. Santa Fe upgraded its passenger-service F3s with stainless-steel Far-Air grilles, replacing the original screen-wire-covered side openings, giving them an appearance much like later F7s. *J. David Ingles*

with water tanks), Baltimore & Ohio (37 As, 7 Bs; 30 of the As were paired with other As equipped with water tanks), Southern and subsidiaries (20 As, 22 Bs), Union Pacific (14 Bs) Northern Pacific (9 As, 7 Bs), Erie (14 As, 7 Bs), Lackawanna (10 As, 5 Bs), Missouri Pacific (10 As, 10 Bs), Atlantic Coast Line (12 F2As, 12 F2Bs), Great Northern (30 As, 14 Bs), Nashville, Chattanooga & St. Louis (12 Bs), and Western Pacific (3 As, 6 Bs).

Variations

During its production, the F3 received several mechanical upgrades to the engine, electrical system, and various components. This resulted in a number of significant visible detail changes to the body. Although to EMD all these variations were still just the 1,500-hp F3, railfans and modelers wanted a way to identify these changes. The result is what have become known as "Phases." Pioneered by the locomotive newsmagazine *Extra 2200 South,* these are not official designations but have become widely accepted as a method of telling the variations apart. (Similar designations have been applied to many other locomotives since the F3.)

The production run of F3s is grouped

Louisville & Nashville no. 2501 is a Phase III F3 built in August 1948. The railroad had two F3As and three F3Bs, all with low-speed 65:12 (45 mph) gearing. An A-B-B set is shown just after delivery in the railroad's "black cat" scheme. *Trains magazine collection*

Pennsylvania Railroad no. 9543 is a Phase IV F3 built in October 1948. The distinctive fabricated stainless-steel grille distinguishes these locomotives from earlier F3s, giving them an appearance similar to an early F7. The railings atop the roof are antennas for the railroad's TrainPhone induction radio system. The locomotive has the closed (straight) "passenger-style" pilot. *Electro-Motive Division*

into four basic Phases, with some additional subgroups and variations (modelers and railfans looking for information on specific locomotive numbers or orders are wise to check roster information, specific delivery dates, and photos when possible). The first F3s already described were Phase I F3s: these are easily identified by their three side portholes and radiator fans with high-profile shrouds. They were built until June 1947.

The first change came at that time. The center porthole was eliminated on the A unit, with four small rectangular openings for engine air intakes and filters added to the side panels between the two remaining portholes. The entire area between the portholes between the batten strips was covered by screen wire (sometimes called "chicken wire," but it was a sturdier screen more resembling chain link). The rearmost upper screened opening was also made longer.

At the same time, the standard number boards were changed from small side-mounted versions to large 45-degree boxes mounted at the corners of the nose (although the smaller number boards remained a buyer option through F3 production). This body style became known as the Phase II early (or Phase IIa) F3, and

An A-B-B set of Atlantic Coast Line F3s with white flags flying rolls an extra freight northward toward Richmond, Va., in February 1953. Lead locomotive 342 and its B units are Phase IV F3s, delivered in December 1948.
Bob Milner

From this angle, Burlington Phase IV F3 no. 135, built in November 1948, is indistinguishable from an early F7. It has a fabricated stainless grill on the top of the side and louvered panels covering the air intakes. Burlington preferred closed passenger-style pilots on its F units. The conduit between the windshields runs up to the rooftop radio antenna.
Chicago, Burlington & Quincy

this remained the basic appearance into December 1947.

A variation came starting in December 1947 with a change to a new style of low-profile rooftop fans. Gone were the high shrouds, making it easy to tell from trackside (or side-on photos) which ones were on a locomotive. A caution for modelers is that, because of the modular nature of these fans, as the locomotives aged, early locomotives sometimes received low-profile versions as replacements and newer locomotives could get rebuilt high fans (and many locomotives have been photographed with some of each). Built through July 1948, these were known as Phase II late or Phase IIb F3s.

Above left: This rear view of a Burlington F3B shows the hostler's window found on B units with hostler controls (which allow operating the B on its own). You can also see the small horn, backup light, MU and brake hoses, and diaphragm. The engine is CB&Q no. 166B (former 138C), a Phase IV F3B built in October 1948. *Louis A. Marre collection*

Above right: Chicago Great Western F3 113A and several sister F units wait at Chicago for their next westbound assignment. Number 113A is a Phase IV F3 built in February 1949; it was among the final F3s built before production switched to F7s. *C. Zeiler*

The next major body change to the F3A came in July 1948 when the screen wire covering the area between portholes was replaced by solid panels, but with four sets of horizontal louvers covering the air-intake filters. These are Phase III F3s.

The final body style emerged in September 1948, with a side-length stainless-steel grille covering the upper body openings (these are described in Chapter 4). Through F3 production, these grilles were fabricated, with horizontal slats across a series of vertical support posts. The horizontal members have four heavy frame pieces, dividing the grill into three sections, with five narrow horizontal pieces in each section. The grilles were installed as three separate panels on A units (with a 6-6-6 pattern) and four panels on B units (5-6-6-6 pattern). These were Phase IV F3s, and this is the body used until the end of F3 production in February 1949.

Most of the body changes were made to improve circulation issues for both radiator intake air and engine combustion air. The biggest mechanical change during F3 production was the move from the D17 to the D27 traction motor in late 1948, which gave the locomotive a much-improved short-time rating (more on that in Chapter 6).

In fact, at that time EMD originally planned to rebrand the locomotive as a new model, the F5 (about the same time as the Phase IV body appeared). However, after the engineering department proposal, the sales department decided that not enough had changed to warrant a new model designation. The result was that production continued as the F3. Although the F5 designation appeared on a lot of official EMD paperwork and proposals—and some modelers and railfans refer to the Phase IV F3 as an F5—EMD was specific in that it never became a separate model. A note on the summary page of section 2 of EMD's *Locomotive Reference Data* books (EMD's periodical record books of all locomotive orders and sales) states, "All F5 locomotives were delivered as F3 units."

Cab-unit sales were going strong, and the next step in 1949 would be an upgrade to the F7, which would become EMD's best-selling carbody diesel.

CHAPTER 6

THE FINAL FREIGHT CABS

THE F7 AND F9 EASED THE TRANSITION TO ROAD SWITCHERS

Six-month-old 462A leads an A-B-B-A consist of F7s on a Great Northern freight near Klamath Falls, Ore., in July 1953. Included in the train are two new GP7s being delivered. The F7 would become EMD's best-selling cab unit, but the Geeps foretold the future. *Bob Milner*

After a number of improvements across its locomotive line, EMD released a new freight cab locomotive in 1949, the F7. The F7's release coincided with EMD's new passenger diesel, the E8, as well as the company's first true road-switcher, the GP7. Although it wasn't realized at the time, the GP7 would prove to be the beginning of the end for the carbody-style diesel locomotive.

EMD's most-successful cab diesel: the F7

The F7 emerged as a new model in February 1949, and would become EMD's biggest-selling cab diesel, with nearly 3,800 sold (2,316 A units and 1,483 B units) through December 1953. The F7 line would also include a new passenger version, the FP7, with a stretched body that allowed additional steam-generator capacity (more on the FP7 on page 151).

The F7 and its road-switcher cousin, the GP7, largely finished the job of dieselization started by the FT. In 1950—a year into F7 production—there were still significantly more steam locomotives in service than diesels (25,640 to 14,047 on Class 1 railroads) but the gap was closing quickly. The last U.S. steam road locomotives had been built in 1950, and the last reciprocating steam locomotive of any type, an 0-8-0 switcher built by Norfolk & Western, was outshopped in 1953. In 1950 Illinois Central president Wayne Johnston was widely quoted in the trade press saying that the IC—although an EMD customer for E units and switchers—"will not dieselize its freight services for a long time, if ever." A "long time" turned out to be just over a year, as IC began receiving GP7s in 1951. By 1955,

Several F7s are at EMD's LaGrange assembly plant in 1950. The near locomotive shows the 36" fan over the dynamic-brake panel on the roof, just to the right of the four radiator fans. *Electro-Motive Division*

Electro-Motive F7 demonstrator no. 1950 shows that externally the F7 was nearly identical to the last F3s, except for the dynamic brake fan on the roof (replacing screened openings). *Electro-Motive Division*

Chicago & North Western no. 4071C is one of the first F7s built, delivered in March 1949. The large number boxes became standard on F7s. The locomotive wears the railroad's as-delivered green, yellow, and black scheme. *Chicago & North Western*

Above: New York Central F7 no. 1709 and two Geeps get ready to head a freight train at West Detroit on a cold New Year's Day 1962. The 1709 was built in June 1951 and still wears the NYC's lightning-stripe scheme. *J. David Ingles*

Opposite top: Santa Fe relied on F units for most passenger trains, with passenger units wearing the red and silver warbonnet scheme. Number 303 is an early F7, built in October 1949, and has 56:21 (102 mph) gearing. On Santa Fe, passenger A units carried extra water (the fill hatch is above the frame just behind the rear side door), while the B units had steam generators. *Santa Fe*

a year after F7 production ended, the Class 1 locomotive tally had turned to 24,786 diesels and 5,982 steam engines.

Mechanically, the F7 was essentially the same as the GP7. The GP7 wound up being extremely successful (2,734 built), and although the F7 outsold it by a thousand copies, by the early 1950s the road switcher was gaining rapidly in popularity and F unit sales began dropping.

The biggest mechanical upgrade to the F7 was the new D27 traction motor, an earlier version of which first appeared on late F3s. The new motor had better materials and insulation, giving it dramatically better resistance to damage from heat from overloading. The F7 had the same horsepower rating (1,500) as the F3, but with a higher tonnage rating and much-improved electrical load ratings. The continuous motor rating went from 700 to 825 amps (the load at which the motors could continually operate without damage), and the short-time rating also improved,

ELECTRO-MOTIVE F7

This drawing shows a Phase I F7, with early fabricated grille, 36" dynamic brake fan, rear roof overhang, rounded door corners, and small cab windows. Body features later changed, but overall dimensions remained the same. *Kalmbach Media*

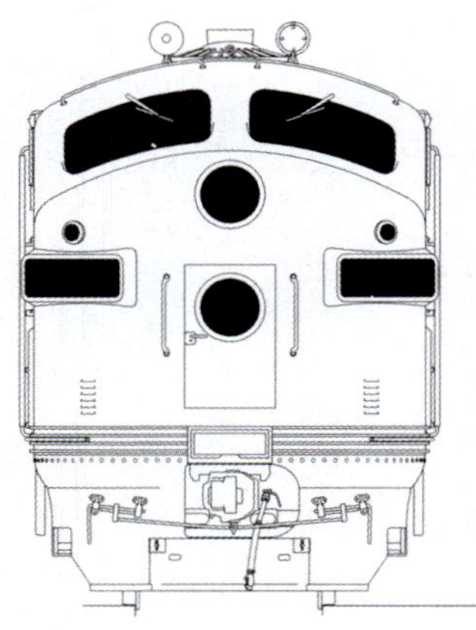

9'-0"
10'-8"
30'-0"
10'-0"
18"
50'-8"

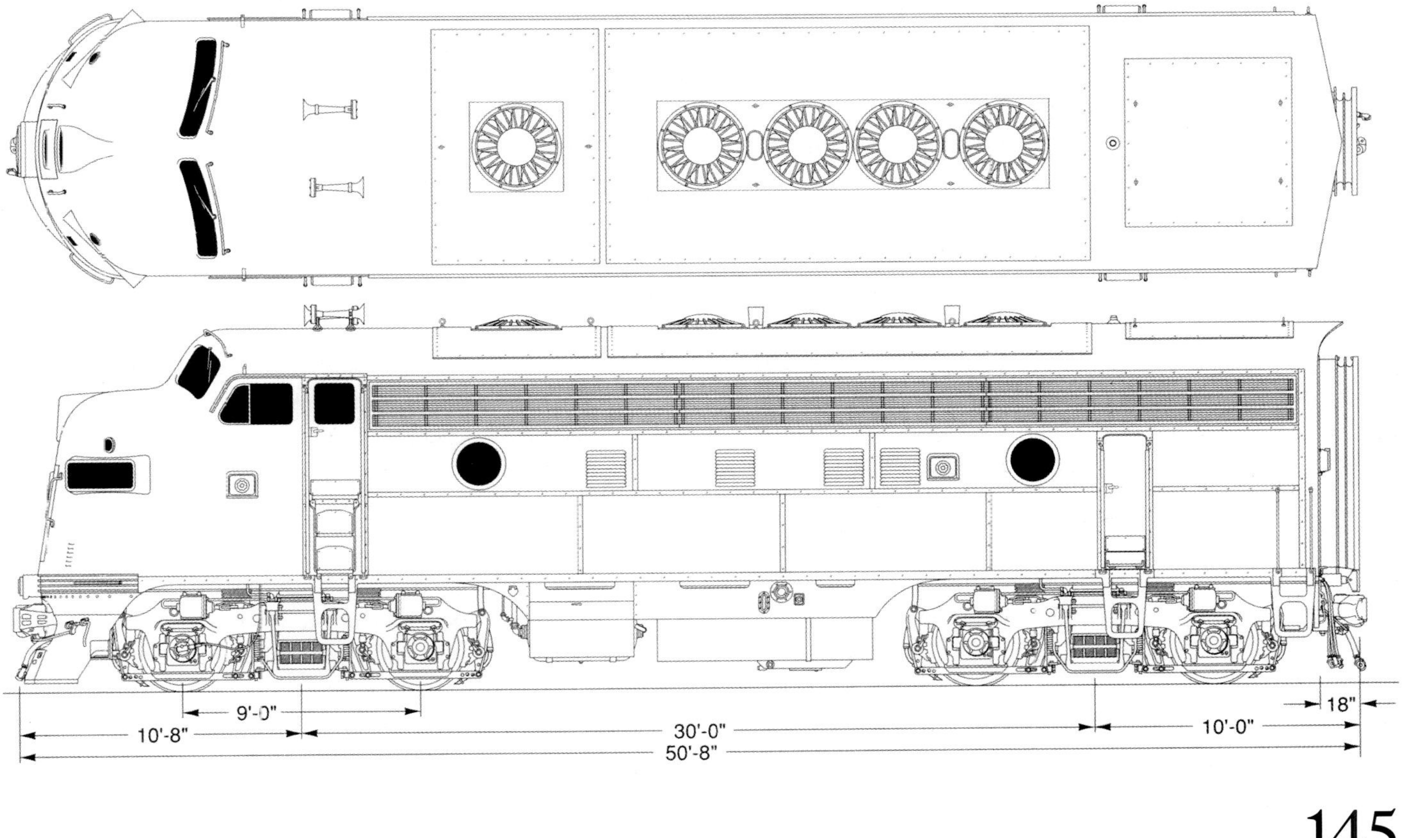

Santa Fe no. 260C, built in August 1951, is an oddball: it's an F7, but it (along with no. 259) was delivered without stainless grilles, giving it the look of an F3. It's wearing the railroad's blue and yellow freight scheme, leading a matched six-unit consist at Vaughn, N.M., in January 1964.
J. David Ingles

effectively boosting the tonnage rating about 25 percent.

Another F7 feature was an improved dynamic brake, which resulted in the addition of a rooftop fan atop the dynamic brake grid on the forward roof panel (the 36" fan was identical to the four radiator fans). This was the only visible external change; otherwise the first F7s were identical in appearance to the last (Phase IV) F3s. Other body details remained the same, including the fabricated grille atop the side and louvers covering the engine-air intake filters.

As with the F3, several railroads opted for F7s as passenger locomotives, with the steam generator at the rear of the body identifiable by the vent and stack atop the rear roof panel.

A number of body details changed during F7 production, although the variations were not as dramatic as with the F3. The initial F7s are known as Phase I early (or Phase Ia) bodies. The first change came in March 1951, with locomotives receiving stamped-metal Far-Air grilles (technically Far-Air Dynamic Grilles, made by the Farr Co.), replacing the earlier fabricated design. This was a change made on E8s at the same time (more on Far-Air grilles in Chapter 4). The new grilles are easily spotted by their three rows of vertical slits.

The cab doors were revised, with rounded corners (earlier locomotives had doors with square corners), and they no longer had separate metal kick plates at the bottom. The end doors were given a round window instead of square one in November 1950. The side cab windows (forward of the door) became taller (just by 2", but noticeable) with a rounded corner, in June 1951. This was known as a Phase I late body, although some of the features vary by date.

The next major change came in February 1952, with the Phase II body. The side panels over the air-intake filters received two sets of vertically stamped louvers, replacing the original horizontal-louver design. In August 1952, dynamic-brake-equipped F7s began receiving larger (48"-diameter) fans on the forward roof hatch. The rear roof overhang was eliminated in October 1952. Another change loved by crews was the switch from sand-fill hatches with round opening knobs ("knuckle busters") to a simple pull-down hinge design, with a

Chicago, Burlington & Quincy's F units were known as "graybacks." Number 165A is an early F7, built in May 1951. It has a distinctive "wagon wheel" radio antenna, and has had its fuel-tank shroud removed by the time of this mid-1960s photo.
Hol Wagner collection

Chicago Great Western no. 153 is an early F7, built in June 1949 for passenger service. The CGW relied on steam-generator-equipped Fs for its passenger trains, but they used standard freight gearing (62:15, 65 mph) as its trains did not have fast schedules. The scene is Omaha, Neb., in the late 1950s.
R.R. Wallin collection

Santa Fe laborers C.T. Krisol and L.J. Hollis add water (left hose) and diesel fuel to passenger F units during a stop at the Argentine (Kansas City) fuel rack in November 1954. *Santa Fe*

Erie F7 no. 711 leads a westbound freight out of Maybrook (N.Y.) yard. The 711A/B/C/D set was built in January 1950 and delivered in the black and yellow scheme. The Erie opted for single headlights on A units, and the firecracker antenna above the cab marks a radio-equipped unit. *Jim Shaughnessy*

An A-B-A set of Milwaukee Road F7s leads a southbound freight toward Indiana in July 1952. Number 69A was built in July 1950. *Bob Milner*

NORTH OF THE BORDER: GENERAL MOTORS DIESEL LTD.

By the 1940s, EMD was looking to expand its sales to Canadian railroads. Even though the country hosted a pioneering road diesel in the 1920s, Canada largely remained a steam holdout well into the 1940s. The first EMD sales north of the border were switchers to Canadian National and Toronto, Hamilton & Buffalo in 1946, then six F3s to CN in 1948 and a trio of E8s to Canadian Pacific in 1949. Exporting locomotives to Canada was difficult because of import taxes and regulations.

The solution was to establish a new division and build a manufacturing plant in Canada, which EMD did in London, Ontario. The factory opened in August 1950 and outshopped its first diesels (GP7s for TH&B) later that month. The new division was known as General Motors Diesel Ltd., or GMD. The factory built switchers, Geeps, and F units (but no E units: the only Canadian Es were the three earlier CP E8s). The locomotives built by GMD sometimes varied in details compared to those built in the U.S., but the mechanical specifications were the same for F7s, FP7s, F9s, and FP9s.

Along with locomotives for Canadian railroads, GMD built export locomotives as well. By 1960, when F unit production had ended, GMD had turned out more than 1,800 diesel locomotives.

Denver & Rio Grande Western F7 set no. 558 was built in May 1949. Individual units would soon be renumbered 5581, 5582, 5583, and 5584. These are freight units; D&RGW also had passenger-service F3s, F7s, and F9s.
Electro-Motive Division

square opening and small horizontal handle.

With any of these detail changes, dates may vary and overlap depending upon where locomotives were in the production process and when specific subassemblies were put together. Check photos and specific rosters for accurate information.

The last cab-unit series: the F9

The last freight F unit was the F9, with first deliveries in January 1954. Its introduction coincided with the E9 passenger cab unit and the GP9 road switcher. It represented another significant upgrade, with the 567C engine (with individual cylinder-liner water jumpers and an improved manifold). The design improved efficiency and eliminated issues with fluid leakage on older versions, and had a higher maximum engine speed (835 rpm compared to 800 rpm), all of which boosted the output to 1,750 hp. The traction motors were again upgraded, to the D37 design. This boosted the tonnage rating, increased the reliability, and almost eliminated the short-term rating for all but maximum amperage levels, meaning the F9 would be limited more by adhesion than motor limits.

Louisville & Nashville F7As 806 and 808 lead a 106-car southbound freight near Montgomery, Ala., in May 1955. The F7s were built in May 1950. *J. Parker Lamb, Jr.*

Kansas City Southern F7s 32A, 32B, and 33A were technically owned by subsidiary Louisiana & Arkansas. The red, yellow, and black units were among the first F7s built, in February 1949, and were equipped for passenger service with steam generators and high-speed (58:19) 89-mph gearing. *Electro-Motive Division*

Automatic transition became standard on the F9 (it had become an option during F3 production), simplifying operation. Transition is the electrical shifting of traction motors from series to parallel as amperage increases and decreases (see page 118 for details), something that had to be done manually on early Fs.

Mechanically the F9 was virtually the same as the GP9 road switcher. However, unlike the F7, which outsold its GP7 cousin, the F9 trailed the GP9 significantly in sales (4,157 to 312). By the early 1950s, railroads had become sold on the road switcher design for its bi-directional visibility and operational capability, flexibility, ease of assembling locomotive consists, and better maintenance access. As a result, only 151 F9As and 161 F9Bs units were built for 20 railroads until F unit production ended in May 1957. Northern Pacific was by far the biggest customer, buying 38 A units and 32 Bs.

Nashville, Chattanooga & St. Louis owned 23 F7As and eight F7Bs. Number 830, shown at Memphis, Tenn., in April 1956, was built in March 1951. It has had part of its fuel-tank shroud removed. *Louis A. Marre collection*

Visually, the F9 retained most details of late F7s, but with the addition of a fifth louvered air intake ahead of the forward porthole on each side, with the porthole location moved back slightly. The headlight lens also became flush instead of slightly recessed (as with the E9—see page 111).

Dual-service FP7 and FP9

Most railroads that operated Fs in passenger service paired A units and B units, taking advantage of the full-size (1,200-gallon) water supply tank of the B unit. In many cases—especially in cold weather or with long trains—railroads would add an extra B unit or two just for the increased water capacity.

Many secondary and smaller passenger trains would be served well by an F, but didn't justify an added B unit (or a single E unit). To serve this market, EMD came up with a new design, the FP7, with increased

Rock Island F7A 121 and F7B 677B pause at Des Moines, Iowa, in May 1959. The 121, in the red and black freight scheme, was built in May 1951; no. 677B wears passenger red and silver, has a steam generator, and was built in March 1949. *Jeff Wilson collection*

Northern Pacific's passenger F units wore a two-tone green scheme with white striping. Here F7 no. 6509C and an F9 A-B are at Livingston, Mont., in May 1967. Built in September 1949, it had a 3,000-pound steam generator and 80-mph (59:18) gearing.
J. David Ingles collection

steam-generator water capacity compared to a standard F7.

It's important to understand that an FP7 was not simply a steam-generator-equipped F7—the FP7 is a specific model, with a body 4 feet longer than a standard F7. The wheelbase was also stretched 4 feet, to 34 feet. This allowed an additional 820-gallon water tank beyond the capacity of a standard F7. Another point to remember is that FP7s were only A units—there's no such thing as an FP7 B unit (since standard F7Bs already had space for a water tank).

At first glance the two models appear very similar, but the FP7 has a longer space between the forward porthole and the first

Texas & Pacific no. 1500 was among the first F7s built, in February 1949. It had side number boards, dual headlights, nose ladder grabs, and grab irons above the windows.
Electro-Motive Division

Snow is falling as Wabash train KB-6 passes the interlocking tower at Jacksonville, Ill., behind F7As 622, 723, and 656 in February 1964. Wabash owned 118 F7As but just nine F7Bs. *J. David Ingles*

Western Maryland F7 no. 61, built in November 1950, is at Oakwood Yard on Norfolk & Western's former Wabash line into Detroit in 1973. The Union Pacific SD40s are on a run-through freight from Kansas City.
J. David Ingles

An A-B set of F7s lead a Baltimore & Ohio freight in the mid-1950s. The railroad was a major operator of F7s, with 157 A units and 100 F7Bs. Number 365 was built in December 1950.
Bob Milner

A matched set of five warbonnet-painted Santa Fe F7s leads a passenger train westbound over the diamonds at Ash Street in Chicago in the mid-1960s. Number 313 is a Phase II F7 built in March 1953. The Fs have 56:21 gearing, allowing a top speed of 102 mph. *Craig Willett*

Denver & Rio Grande Western no. 5711 is a late F7, built in June 1952. It has Far-Air grilles over the upper side openings, vertical-slit louvers over the side air intakes between portholes, rounded doors, and rounded-corner side cab windows.
Electro-Motive Division

Great Northern train 30, an all-stops Crookston, Minn., to St. Paul local, pulls out of Fergus Falls, Minn., in May 1953. The lead F7, 280A, was built in June 1952. It's a Phase II version, with vertical louvers and Far-Air grilles. *George Krambles; Krambles-Peterson Archives*

louvered air intake. Also, the FP7's side grille had an extra short section added, giving it a 6-2-6-6 pattern. Other body details changed during production following the lead of the F7.

The FP7 was intended as a dual-service (freight/passenger) locomotive, but how they were used varied by railroad. Some railroads bought them strictly for passenger service; others intended to use them for both, or just as backup passenger power when needed. The gear ratio chosen by each railroad reflected that intent (its suitability for pairing with other Fs in freight service was dependent upon the gearing of each).

A total of 378 FP7s were built from June 1949 through December 1953. They went to 28 railroads, including 18 for National of Mexico, plus two export engines to Saudi Arabia. The three largest customers were Louisville & Nashville (45), Atlantic Coast Line (44), and Pennsylvania Railroad (40).

The basic model would continue as the FP9 with the change to the F9, but it was not as popular: 86 FP9s were built, but only 4 for a U.S. railroad. These were for Chicago & North Western, and they were rebuilt from FTs and designated FP9m, as they were only rated at 1,500 hp. Canadian roads got more than half of FP9s built:

Four F7As lead a New York Central freight at Collinwood, Ohio, in August 1964. The lead F7, no. 1743, is a Phase II engine built in April 1952; it still wears its original lightning-stripe scheme. The second unit is an earlier F7 (note the louver difference); the trailing engines all wear the simplified black scheme. *J. David Ingles*

Soo Line no. 2228B is a late (Phase II) F7, built in August 1953. It's at the railroad's Schiller Park, Ill., engine facility in June 1978. Soo still had 33 of its original 57 F units in operation at that time, but their days were numbered. *Ed DeRouin*

Chesapeake & Ohio no. 7076 is a Phase II F7 built in April 1952. By the 1960s it had been modified with additional grab irons, spark arrestors on the exhaust stacks, and its fuel-tank shroud was removed. The railroad owned 94 F7As and 54 F7Bs. *Chesapeake & Ohio*

Southern Pacific Train 52 (note the train number in the indicator boards), the *San Joaquin Daylight,* rolls to a stop at Madera, Calif., in July 1966. Four F7s are in charge, with no. 6445 leading; it's a Phase II version, built in February 1953. *Craig Willett*

The F9 has an additional louvered engine-air intake ahead of the forward side porthole. Milwaukee Road F9 no. 81C was built in January 1954. It was one of 12 F9s (6 As, 6 Bs) on the railroad. *Electro-Motive Division*

Canadian National (43) and Canadian Pacific (11), with 25 to Mexico and three to Saudi Arabia.

Dual electric/diesel-electric FL9

In the mid-1950s the New York, New Haven & Hartford was looking for a dual-power (electric/diesel-electric) passenger locomotive that it could operate both on its main line (as a standard diesel-electric) and into third-rail electric territory in New York City (as an electric locomotive). Electro-Motive's solution was an adaptation of a locomotive it had designed (but never built) for a lengthened, passenger-specific version of the FP9. The design was basically an FP9 with an even-longer body, with a third-rail shoe and extra electrical gear added to allow it to operate from third-rail power.

Externally the FL9 body looks like an FP9, but is about 4 feet longer (59'-0" compared to 54'-8" for an FP7 or FP9). The extra internal space was used by the steam generator and large water tank along with

Northern Pacific owned far more F9s than any other railroad: 38 F9As and 32 F9Bs. Number 6701A, built in August 1956, shows the large (48"-diameter) dynamic brake fan on the forward roof hatch. The NP opted for dual headlights, nose MU, nose lift rings, and a winterization hatch (above the rear radiator fan). It's at St. Paul, Minn., in July 1960. *Jeff Wilson collection*

additional electrical gear. The body has five engine air intake louvers (four between the portholes, one ahead of the forward porthole) and a Far-Air grille along the top of each side. All were equipped with the distinctive Hancock air whistle instead of a horn, mounted just above and between the windshields.

The biggest variation was the six-wheel truck at the rear, with the center axle unpowered. The truck was a variation of EMD's Flexicoil design, which was quite different compared to the A1A Blomberg truck of E units (which couldn't be fitted with 40"-diameter wheels and didn't have enough clearance to allow pickup shoes). This gave the locomotive a B-A1A wheel arrangement.

Two test units were built in late 1956, but they had issues with fires caused by slow-acting fuses and grounded electrical gear. The third-rail pickup shoes were problematic as they were located only on

ELECTRO-MOTIVE F9

The F9 had the same dimensions as the F7, but with upgraded details including Far-Air grille, vertical-slit louvers in a different arrangement, large (48"-diameter) dynamic brake fan, and no rear roof overhang.
Kalmbach Media

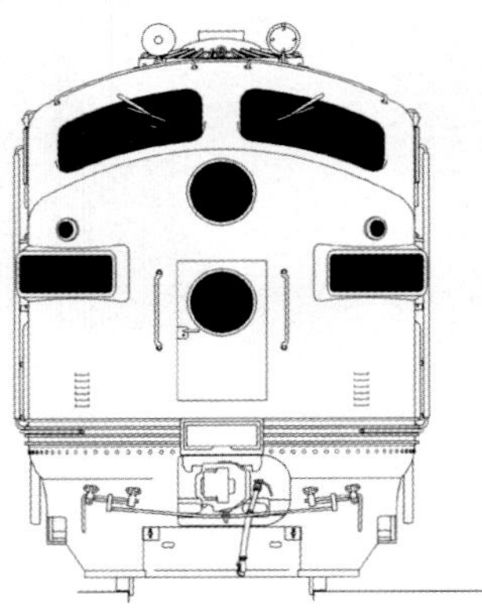

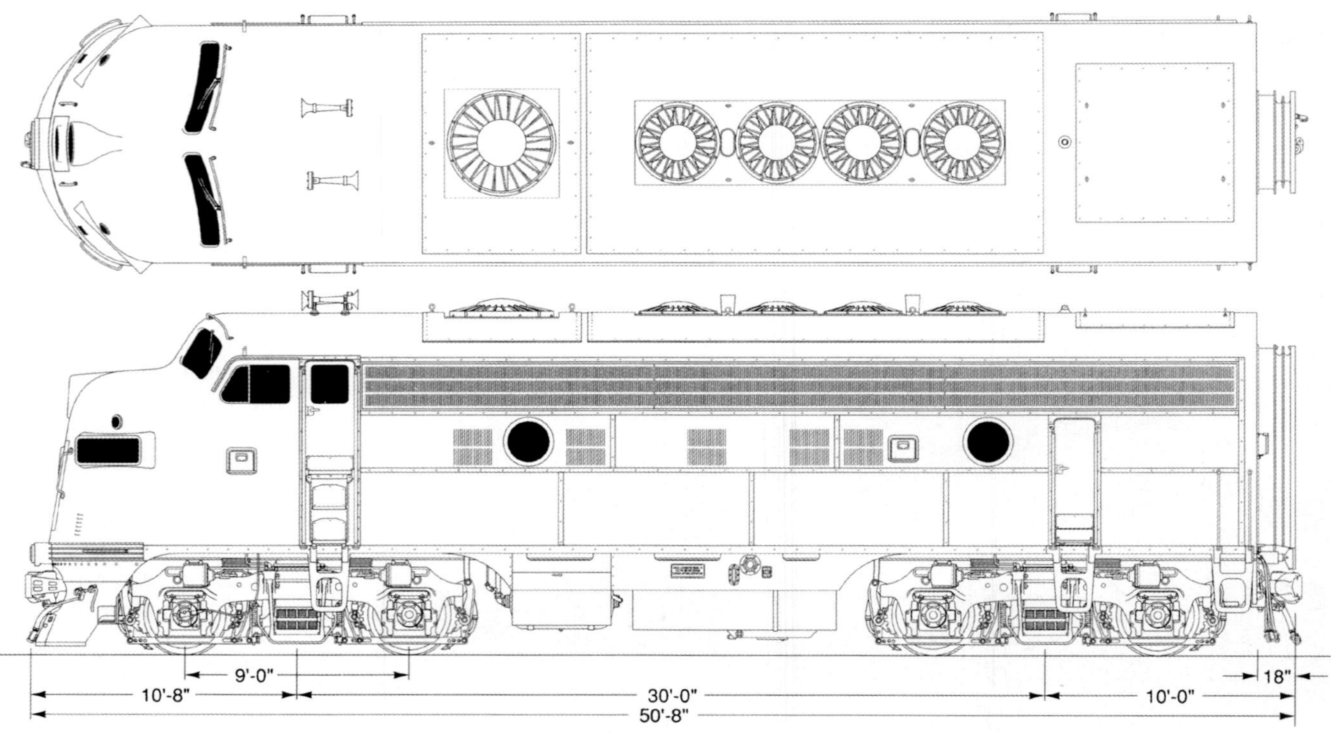

F7 AND F9 PRODUCTION

F7 • February 1949-December 1953			
ACL	76	12	3/50-12/51
Alaska	5	4	12/52-12/53
ATSF	215	247	6/49-12/53
B&LE	28	26	6/50-2/53
B&O	157	100	8/49-1/53
B&M	4	4	3/49-11/50
C&NW	88	18	3/49-4/50
C&O	94	54	9/50-11/52
C&S	6	6	8/50
C&WC	6	0	12/50
CB&Q	10	3	5/50
CGW	4	19	6/49-5/51
Clinch	15	11	3/49-12/52
CN	58	18	8/51-11/52
CP	0	29	9/51-2/53
CRI&P	31	17	3/49-5/51
D&RGW	44	42	2/49-7/52
DL&W	9	6	7/49
Erie	6	6	1/50-3/51
FW&D	6	6	8/50
GM&O	4	10	9/49-7/50
GN	62	46	4/49-2/53
KCS	17	21	2/49-4/51
KO&G	4	2	4/49
L&N	69	17	4/50-6/51
LV	8	6	2/50-1/51
M&StL	8	0	11/49-12/50
MILW	68	50	5/49-4/53
MKT	16	8	6/49-2/52
MP	50	12	9/49-3/51
NdeM	25	16	11/49-12/51
NC&StL	23	8	4/49-3/51
NP	45	34	4/49-2/52
NYC	238	55	5/49-10/52
PRR	123	76	4/49-9/52
RDG	18	6	5/50
RF&P	10	10	11/49-2/50
SLSF	22	22	3/49-6/53
Soo	26	10	11/49-7/52
SOU	93	54	5/49-11/52
SP	294	236	6/49-7/53
SP&S	4	0	1/53
SSW	26	17	2/50-9/52
T&P	83	35	2/49-8/51
Tex-Mex	2	0	5/49
UP	17	35	3/51-10/52
Wabash	126	9	8/49-1/53
WM	26	14	3/50-12/52
WP	24	26	1/50-6/51
Total:	2,393	1,463	

F9 • January 1954-April 1957			
ACL	2	0	5/57
ATSF	18	18	6/56-7/56
Clinch	0	5	4/55
CN	0	38	12/54-1/57
CP	0	8	1/54-4/54
D&RGW	2	4	9/55
Erie Mng.	5	6	5/56-8/56
GN	0	6	2/54
L&N	8	4	11/56-12/56
MILW	6	6	1/54-11/55
MKT	0	4	3/55
NdeM	10	10	2/54-11/54
NP	38	32	2/54-3/56
SLSF	0	13	1/54-4/57
Total:	89	154	

FP7 • June 1949-December 1953			
A&WP	4	8/49-2/51	
ACL	44	4/51-9/52	
Alaska	3	12/53	
C&EI	10	8/49-9/49	
C&O	16	2/52-12/52	
CGW	2	12/50	
Clinch	1	2/52	
CP	35	9/50-6/53	
CRI&P	10	6/49-7/49	
FEC	5	12/51	
Georgia	3	11/49-2/50	
L&N	45	1/51-1/52	
MILW	32	6/50-9/52	
MKT	8	1/52-2/52	
NdeM	18	12/49-11/51	
NP	2	2/52	
ONR	22	3/51-10/53	
PRR	40	4/52-8/52	
RDG	8	5/50-9/52	
RF&P	3	11/50	
SLSF	12	12/50-2/51	
SSW	1	4/50	
Soo	8	5/49-8/53	
SOU	20	4/50-12/50	
SP	16	2/53-3/53	
UP	2	4/52	
WofA	2	11/49	
WP	4	1/50	
Total:	376		

FP9 • February 1954-December 1959			
C&NW	4*	7/55-11/55	
CN	43	9/54-7/58	
CP	11	2/54-5/54	
NdeM	25	8/56-11/56	
Total:	83		

* FP9m, rebuilt from FTs, 1,500 hp

An A-B-A-B-A set of Santa Fe F units lead a perishable train at Belen, N.M., in January 1964. Leading is F9A 286C, built in July 1956. The largest operator of F units rostered 18 F9As and 18 F9Bs.
J. David Ingles

St. Louis-San Francisco no. 5007 is an F9Am, one of two rebuilt from wreck-damaged F3s in 1954 (5005 was the other). Externally it matches other F9s, with 48" dynamic brake fan and typical grille and louver arrangement. It's at Summit, Calif., on the Santa Fe in run-through service in February 1962.
Chard Walker

Soo Line no. 500A is an FP7, former EMD demonstrator 9051 built in November 1949. The extra 4 feet of length is apparent in the added space between the forward porthole and first louver set, and in the gap under the frame behind the lead truck. Both it and the 500B, a steam-generator-equipped F7B, have winterization hatches.
Electro-Motive Division

Southern FP7 3496 was built as no. 6130 in April 1950 and is shown here at Atlanta in 1984. It had 58:19 gearing for a top speed of 89 mph. Southern opted for a multi-chime horn, single headlight, and added spark arrestors atop the exhaust stacks. *George W. Hamlin*

Reading owned eight FP7s (nos. 900-907). Number 901, built in May 1950, has the same spotting features as Phase I F7s: fabricated (horizontal-slit) upper side grille, horizontal louver openings, and rounded cab doors. The locomotive is black with green and yellow striping.
Electro-Motive Division

St. Louis Southwestern FP7 no. 306 pauses at Mount Pleasant, Texas, with Train 107 bound for Dallas in September 1954. The SSW (nicknamed the Cotton Belt Route) owned just one FP7, no. 306, built in April 1950 and painted in parent Southern Pacific's *Daylight* passenger scheme.
R.S. Plummer; Louis A. Marre collection

the rear truck, which wasn't sufficient to bridge gaps in the third rail at crossings and turnouts. The two were rebuilt, with two-axle Flexicoil trucks at the front with pickup shoes, an upgraded electrical fix, and small pantographs on the roof.

The reconfigured locomotives worked well enough that New Haven bought 60 FL9s in two 30-unit orders. The first arrived from late 1956 to November 1957 (the two test units plus 28 production locomotives); the next batch were the last F units built, delivered from September to November 1960. The first batch had the 567C engine (same as the F9) and were rated at 1,750 hp; the second batch the 567D1 (also used in the GP18), rated at 1,800 hp.

The locomotives were not a resounding success, but allowed New Haven to retire its aging Alco DL-109 passenger diesels and

Rock Island FP7 no. 402 was built in June 1949. It was one of 10 on the railroad (nos. 402-411), delivered in the passenger scheme of red, black, and silver. They had the same gearing (61:16, 70 mph) as freight-service F7s. *Electro-Motive Division*

Milwaukee Road purchased 32 FP7s, including no. 92C, built in July 1950. The Milwaukee opted for closed (passenger-style) pilots and dual headlights. Five, including 92C, had freight (62:15, 65 mph) gearing; the rest had high-speed 58:19 (89 mph) gearing. *Electro-Motive Division*

Canadian Pacific FP7 no. 4062 and a steam-generator-equipped F7B lead a train in the Canadian Rockies in a publicity photo. Number 4062, built in 1952, was one of 35 FP7s built for CP by EMD subsidiary General Motors Diesel Ltd. (GMD) in Canada. *Canadian Pacific*

several older classes of electrics, and they operated well enough that several became the last F units in regular mainline service, with some being rebuilt and running into the 2000s.

End of an era

The FL9s proved to be the last F units built. However, prolific rail author and diesel expert Preston Cook, who worked at EMD in the 1970s, reports that EMD in the late 1950s did preliminary design work for an F unit that would have continued the series after the F9. The locomotive would have been based on the builder's contemporary road switchers that followed the GP9: the non-turbocharged 1,800-hp GP18 and turbocharged 2,000-hp GP20.

Canadian National was the leading owner of FP9s, with 43. Locomotives built by GMD in Canada often differed slightly in details compared to those built at LaGrange. On the FP9, for example, Canadian FP9s retained horizontal louver sets. Number 6510 was built in January 1955. *Canadian National*

Canadian Pacific had 11 FP9s, including no. 1415. They had unique framed upper grilles, which had a different appearance compared to Far-Air grilles. They also retained horizontal-slit louvers and old-style sand fill hatches. *Canadian Pacific*

The declining sales of streamlined units (Es and Fs) meant that they likely would not be worth the cost of developing and producing them, and the project was canceled.

By the end of F unit production in 1960, Class 1 railroads had 28,278 diesels and 261 steam locomotives in service. From the introduction of the FT until the last FL9 delivery the percentage of steam engines in service had gone from more than 99 percent to less than 1 percent. During that time, railroads went from employing 1.4 million workers to less than 800,000—largely because of the diesel.

The F unit had largely been responsible for dieselizing freight service, but its fate was sealed—like steam when the FT appeared—when the first GP7 rolled out

Several FP9s survived in passenger service for VIA Rail Canada. Number 6524 is a former Canadian National FP9 built in 1957. It's leading a train with an Alco B unit and a GMD B unit in the late 1970s. *VIA Rail*

Chicago & North Western had the only domestic FP9s: four locomotives rebuilt from FTs in 1955 (nos. 4051A-4054A) and designated FP9m. Limits on the remanufactured components gave them 1,500 hp; they had 57:20 gearing for a 95 mph top speed.
Robert C. Anderson

of LaGrange in 1949. The GP (or Geep) was not as attractive as a streamlined carbody locomotive, but it was a strict case of form following function. The road switcher (also called a "hood unit") was a switching locomotive with a nose added at the end of the cab, riding on road trucks, and mechanically just an F unit on a heavy frame with a walkway around a hood. Most importantly, its engine and other internal components were much more accessible and easier to maintain and rebuild than an E or F unit, and road switchers offered better visibility in either direction.

Electro-Motive's Dick Dilworth, the man behind the design of early diesels, the FT, and also the lead designer of the GP7, thought the road switcher he designed was

National of Mexico bought 25 FP9s, nos. 7010-7034, built in 1956. As with the earlier FP7, the extra body length is apparent in the spacing between the lead porthole and second louver set and by the gap behind the lead truck.
Electro-Motive Division

ugly and that railroads wouldn't want it. Dilworth was dead wrong: railroads wanted road switchers, and in droves. What the 1,500-hp GP7 started, the 1,750-hp GP9—the road switcher equivalent of the F9—completed.

Many F units remained in mainline service through the 1960s, but by the end of that decade, advancing age and the coming of new, more-powerful diesels were taking their toll. Some cab units would continue into the 1970s (as Chapter 7 shows), and a few would be rebuilt, but by the 1980s the era of the F unit had largely passed from the railroad scene.

The last F units built were dual-service (electric/diesel-electric) FL9s for New York, New Haven & Hartford. Number 2033 is from the second order, delivered in late 1960. The FL9 was 4 feet longer than an FP9 and had third-rail electrical pickup shoes on its Flexicoil trucks. A Hancock air whistle is mounted above the windshields.
Electro-Motive Division

The FL9 rode on Flexicoil trucks to provide clearance for the retractable third-rail shoe (Blomberg trucks didn't provide enough space). This is a lead (four-wheel) truck; the rear trucks were six-wheel Flexicoils.
Electro-Motive Division

CHAPTER 7

DEMISE OF E AND F UNITS

MANY RAN THEIR LAST MILES IN AMTRAK AND COMMUTER SERVICE

By the late 1960s, early E units—especially prewar slantnose versions such as this Burlington E5—were rare, and were on limited time with Amtrak on the horizon. Colorado & Southern (Burlington subsidiary) no. 9952A, built as CB&Q 9911A in February 1940, is on the railroad's *Texas Zephyr* in August 1967. It would be traded in to EMD in March 1968 but get new life at the Illinois Railway Museum, where it remains operational. *Craig Willett*

Diesel locomotives have typical service lives of 15 to 20 years—a bit more or less depending upon the success of the particular model. This means most early Es were retired by the mid-1950s and FTs by the late 1950s; most post-war Es and Fs were approaching the end of their operating lifespans by the late 1960s and early 1970s.

With the thousands of F units built, it seemed they were everywhere on mainline trains—a dime a dozen to many, with many photographers ignoring them in the 1940s and 1950s as they sought out remaining steam locomotives. However, the coming of new locomotive models and the tremendous growth in high-horsepower freight diesels in the 1960s—first 2,000-hp diesels, then 3,000-hp locomotives by the late 1960s—doomed most F units to secondary roles. Their carbody design limited their operational practicality—it was difficult to use them in any kind of switching service—and made them more difficult to maintain, with restricted access to the engine and other internal components. They were not ideal rebuilding candidates, unlike early Geeps.

But at least there were still plenty of freight trains that F units could pull. Aging E units faced another challenge, in that the service they were designed and built for was going away. Railroads by the 1960s were losing money on passenger service; the U.S. Mail contracts that made many routes profitable were going away, and railroads were eliminating passenger routes and trains as fast as they could get regulatory approval to do so.

In spite of this, some E and F units were indeed rescued from retirement and scrapping, rebuilt, and found new service, with some lasting into the 2000s.

The disappearing E unit

The last production carbody locomotive was an E unit delivered by EMD in January 1964 (Union Pacific no. 914)—a very late date considering Amtrak was formed just

Railroads often modified their F units as they got older. Rock Island FTs 90 and 90A, built in June 1944, remain drawbarred together in August 1963. The B unit has lost its port-holes, replaced by plain panels, and the fuel-tank shroud has been removed from the A unit. They're paired with two GP7s, a match not yet imagined when they were built. *Frank Tatnall*

It's just a year before Amtrak as Seaboard Coast Line E8 no. 588, along with an E7 and another E8, lead a train in April 1970. The lead engine is former Atlantic Coast Line E8 3049, built in October 1950. The SCL was formed with the merger of ACL and Seaboard Air Line in 1967. *Craig Willett*

Through the 1960s as passenger trains were being discontinued and railroads were losing money on passenger service, maintenance—including paint— was often neglected or deferred. Kansas City Southern E9Am no. 25 is on the *Southern Belle* at Heavener, Okla., in May 1969, looking worse for wear. *Tom Hoffman*

Erie Lackawanna re-wheeled and re-geared several of its E8s for freight service in the late 1960s. A trio of them, led by no. 809, lead a freight train at Pullman Junction, Ill., in June 1972. They served until the Conrail merger in 1976. *Tom Hoffman*

The early days of Amtrak provided a wide mix of road names on locomotives as well as cars. Here a leased Gulf, Mobile & Ohio E7 and Penn Central E8 lead cars lettered for Amtrak and Union Pacific. *Earl Thiel; Tom Swenson collection*

It's October 1972, and Amtrak still has a variety of road names on equipment. This train approaches Alexandria, Va., behind E8 no. 253 in Amtrak colors (ex-Seaboard Coast Line E8 no. 596, built as Seaboard Air Line no. 3057), trailed by a former SCL E7 and an ex-Union Pacific B unit. *Craig Willett*

A crossing guard stands watch as Amtrak E9 no. 421 (former Union Pacific no. 944) leads the *James Whitcomb Riley* across diamonds in pavement at Griffith, Ind., in March 1976. Amtrak would continue to operate E units into the 1980s. *Craig Willett*

seven years later. By that time, railroads were turning to high-horsepower dual-service locomotives for passenger service—these were basically modified existing freight locomotives with high-speed gearing and steam generators. Electro-Motive began offering its SDP35 in 1964 (a 2,500-hp, six-axle SD35 with a steam generator) and would follow with the 3,000-hp SDP40 and 3,600-hp SDP45. The advantage to these was that if and when passenger service disappeared, they could be regeared and reassigned to freight service.

For railroads that still wanted streamlined carbodies, EMD would soon offer the FP45, a cowl-bodied SDP45 (and GE offered the U30CG, a cowl-bodied version of its 3,000-hp, six-axle U30C). Although streamlined and smooth-bodied, these were vastly different locomotives compared to E units. They are more accurately "cowl" units as opposed to carbody locomotives, since their outer sheathing is cosmetic and not structural (unlike with the E units' side-girder construction). New passenger diesels would later emerge, but that's a story for a different book.

For many E units, the end of the line came as passenger trains were discontinued. By the 1960s, most railroads were losing money on passenger service and didn't want to spend any more money than needed to keep their E units running. Many finished their careers with peeling and faded paint.

Most early Es (including E3s and E6s) were retired and traded in (scrapped) by the early 1960s, as newer Es were more powerful, more reliable, and there were plenty of them around to cover remaining passenger routes. By the mid-1960s, even the venerable E7 was shrinking rapidly in number as E8s and E9s took over most assignments. Most E7s were retired by 1971.

The E7 and earlier E units served well, proved durable, and railroads certainly got their money's worth from most of them, with many racking up high mileage totals. It should be no surprise that it was an E6, Atlantic Coast Line no. 501, that eventually totaled 5,250,212 miles—then the record for highest-total-mileage locomotive according to EMD—when it was retired on the eve of Amtrak in 1970.

With passenger trains disappearing,

Many E units led extended lives in suburban commuter service, including a group of Burlington Northern (former Chicago, Burlington & Quincy) E8s and E9s serving the former CB&Q line westward from Chicago. They were rebuilt to E9Ams in the mid-1970s; by this March 1992 photo they were nearing retirement. *Jeff Wilson*

Chicago & North Western used both E and F units in its Chicago-area commuter service. Here F7 no. 4080C is on a mid-day "Scoot" on the west line to Geneva, Ill., at Tower A2 in Chicago in 1967. Number 4080C was built in October 1949. *J. David Ingles*

Chicago & North Western rebuilt six former Union Pacific E8 and E9 B units with cabs and noses (nos. 501-506) for commuter service. They were known as "Crandall Cabs" after their designer. Number 504 (ex-UP E8B 935B) is at Des Plaines, Ill., in May 1979. *Jim Hediger*

railroads tried to find other uses for their newer E units, some of which were barely 10 to 12 years old. An A1A-A1A, twin-engined passenger-service diesel, designed to haul fairly light trains at high speeds, is not readily suitable for other types of service. Its idler axles (the center unpowered axles on each truck) help give it a smooth, stable ride at high speeds, but take away from tractive effort, unlike a four- or six-axle freight locomotive where all axles are powered. Since E units were geared for speed, their starting tractive effort was more limited. Their smaller wheel size (36" diameter vs. 40" for an F) meant they couldn't use the same gear ratios as their freight cousins, and the design of the six-wheel Blomberg truck didn't allow swapping in 40" wheels.

If used in freight service, E units were realistically limited to operating in multiple with other E units; running an E with a freight diesel would result in vastly different power and gear ratios; at high speeds it was possible but problematic, but with E units' higher minimum speeds, having one lugging a heavy train at low speed with a freight diesel could damage the E's traction motors quickly.

Some railroads experimented with E units in fast-freight and piggyback service, including Pennsylvania (later Penn Central), Burlington, Erie Lackawanna, Rock Island, Seaboard Air Line, and Union Pacific. The EL went so far in the late 1960s as to replace the original 36" wheels on several of their E8s with 38" wheels (the largest that would work in the A1A Blomberg trucks) and assigned several of them specifically for freight service by re-gearing them at 62:15. This lowered their maximum speed to 62 mph, but also dropped the minimum continuous speed to 16 mph (compared to 29 mph for a standard 57:20 passenger unit), which—although far from ideal—made them much more suitable for heavy loading. Their steam generators were removed and weight added to increase traction. The changes worked well enough that the E8s remained in freight service on the EL until the Conrail merger in 1976.

However, most railroads that tried carrying freight with Es were not as successful, doing it briefly before trading in locomotives. More typical was the experience of Chicago, Burlington & Quincy subsidiary Colorado & Southern, which used consists of E5s to haul freight on grades between Denver and Pueblo, Colo., in a short-lived 1967 experiment. Burned-out traction motors and damaged generators ended the operations after a few months; the E5s were traded in later that year.

Amtrak and commuter service

Amtrak was a double-edged sword for E units upon its formation on May 1, 1971: Its startup meant many trains were eliminated, lowering the total number of passenger locomotives needed; but Amtrak needed many locomotives, so many Es were saved and served several additional years until Amtrak could afford new locomotives.

Amtrak limited its E unit acquisitions to

Rock Island F7 no. 676 leads a Chicago-area commuter train in October 1966. Built in March 1949, it's one of three F7As the Rock purchased with steam generators and high-speed (59:18; 80 mph) gearing. *Craig Willett*

It's three months into the Amtrak era as four former Northern Pacific F9s (two repainted in Burlington Northern colors) lead the *Empire Builder* in August 1971. *Craig Willett*

the latest models (E8s and E9s), and then bought what it felt were the best of what was available, purchasing 216 of them (about a third of the total of those models built) upon startup. (Amtrak also bought 32 F units). Although it did not purchase any E7s, Amtrak did, however, lease some E7s in its first couple of years of operation.

Amtrak began retiring Es a few years later as new six-axle SDP40Fs began arriving in 1973. However, problems with that locomotive, and the resulting switch to the four-axle F40PH design (which didn't begin arriving until 1975), meant plenty of E units lasted on Amtrak until the late 1970s (80 as of 1978), and some made it into the 1980s. Several were rebuilt with HEP units (head-end power engine/generator sets) replacing steam generators for use with Amfleet equipment.

Three railroads that didn't initially join Amtrak—Rock Island, Southern, and Rio Grande—became known for their E and F unit fleets that labored on, carrying those railroads' trains. The Rock also carried commuters in Chicago and had 22 E units in commuter service into the late 1970s, until they were bumped by new F40PHs. The Rock was known for running the last E6 in regular service, no. 630, until it was retired in the late 1970s; it also had four E7s during this time, among the last of the type in service.

BODY MODIFICATIONS

Railroads often modified individual locomotives or groups of locomotives during their service lives. This could be because of wreck or damage repairs, component upgrading, or rebuilding. These modifications could be simple or extensive; in some cases, changes make it difficult to tell at a glance the exact locomotive model. There were some common alterations made to both E and F units.

On Fs and Es alike, the side body panels were easy to modify and swap because of the panel/batten construction. Side portholes were often eliminated or moved, air-intake louvers could be moved, removed, or added, and the screens and louvers covering side openings were often modified or removed. Far-Air grilles were sometimes added in place of original fabricated grilles.

Multiple-unit (MU) connections were often added to the noses of Es and Fs that didn't originally have them. This could be done with recessed hatches on the nose next to the headlight, but was sometimes done with protruding external boxes.

Headlights were often modified. Lower headlights were added to many locomotives that originally had just a single upper light. Signal lights or moving (Mars) lights were sometimes added, and original lamps were sometimes changed.

The rooftop fans were sometimes modified. Most common was replacing older-style (tall shrouded) fans with new low-profile fans. Sometimes all would be replaced, but it was common to replace just one or two as needed.

The tapered shrouding that covered the top of the fuel tanks (on the side of the body between the trucks) was often removed (completely or in part) on both E and F units.

Grab irons were frequently added to E and F noses after delivery. This usually meant a series of horizontal ladder-style grabs up the left side of the nose, then proceeding across the nose. This provided better access to the windshields for cleaning. Long grabs above windshields were also commonly added.

Radio communication became common in the 1950s, and many locomotives received two-way radios. These can be spotted by their antennas, usually located atop the cab roof (often with a visible conduit running to the roof between the windshields). Common antenna styles of the period included the "wagon wheel" (a circular spoked antenna atop a post) and the "firecracker," a vertical cylindrical antenna atop a small mounting pad.

VIA Rail Canada is a year old as FP9 no. 6535, still in Canadian National colors, switches a car at Ottawa, Ontario. Some FP9s would serve through the 1990s.
George Drury

Matched sets of FTs were rare by the 1960s, so this A-B-B-A consist of Northern Pacific FTs at Portland, Ore., in September 1965 is notable. Each A-B set is still drawbar connected. The NP has added a twin lower headlight, nose lift rings, and nose grab irons to the A units.
Jeff Wilson collection

Southern operated its well-maintained fleet of 17 E8s until turning its passenger trains over to Amtrak in 1979. Most of the Es then went to New Jersey Department of Transportation, with a few retired or donated to museums. Rio Grande operated A-B-B F9s on its *Rio Grande Zephyr* until 1983 and ski train into the 1990s.

North of the border, two of Canadian Pacific's three E8s survived until the formation of VIA Rail in 1978, and continued to serve a couple of years after that.

Chicago's commuter lines were home to a few notable long-lasting groups of E units. Burlington Northern had a group of E8s and E9s that served on Chicago's Metra (former CB&Q Aurora line) from the 1970s until 1992. The 25 ex-CB&Q E units were extensively rebuilt by Morrison-Knudsen in 1973 and 1976. The biggest upgrade was the swap of a single 16-cylinder 645 engine to replace the original twin 12-cylinder 567s. The locomotives also received HEP units and upgraded control equipment.

Designated E9Am, they largely retained their original appearance, minus the side portholes and with a red marker light directly below the headlight (for use when trailing in push-pull service). They were retired in 1992, with some going to MARC (Maryland Area Regional Commuter) service.

Another significant group of E and F units in Chicago commuter service were those of Chicago & North Western on north-side

St. Louis Southwestern FTA no. 923 undergoes rebuilding at Electro-Motive in 1960. Note the Far-Air grille over the top openings. *Electro-Motive Division*

Rebuilt Southern Pacific F7 no. 6378, built in July 1952, was the first to be repainted in the railroad's red and gray (bloody nose) scheme, in July 1958. The SP modified its air intakes, giving it the basic appearance of an F9, but the forward two side air intakes have a framed design, and the front intake is slightly higher. *Southern Pacific*

Work-weary Boston & Maine FT no. 4205 rolls through Buskirk, N.Y., in spring 1956. In just a year the B&M would send its entire fleet of 48 FTs to EMD for "rebuilding" into GP9s. *Jim Shaughnessy*

Regional Transportation Authority (RTA) lines. The railroad had operated many HEP-equipped F units in commuter service beginning in the early 1960s, and rebuilt 20 of them in 1971 at its Oelwein, Iowa, shops. The railroad also had 22 E8s equipped with HEP in the 1960s, and acquired additional Es from Kansas City Southern and Union Pacific in 1970, converting them as well. The railroad began rebuilding E units at Oelwein (turning out 11 of them in 1974), but discontinued the program when it became apparent new RTA locomotives would eventually be arriving.

Burlington Northern inherited more than 200 F units from its predecessor railroads at the time of its 1970 merger. Number 720 is an F7, ex-Northern Pacific no. 6010A. Shown here in the late 1970s, it was built in February 1950 and retired in November 1981. *Steve Glischinski*

EMD TEST-BED 462

Electro-Motive maintained several locomotives that it used for testing. In 1960, EMD took a retired F7 (Chicago & North Western no. 6501A, originally built in 1949) and rebuilt it, using it as a test locomotive (or "test bed") for engines and other equipment. Among other duties, no. 462 was used to test EMD's new 645 engine in the early 1960s, and also tested an early alternator (alternators would eventually replace generators from the 1960s through the 1970s). The locomotive showed up on many railroads (but tended to stay in the Midwest), wore a variety of paint schemes over the years, and was often seen with EMD's dynamometer car or test cars from various railroads. It was eventually scrapped in the 1990s.

Electro-Motive used a traded-in F unit as a test bed for various equipment. In this 1962 view, no. 462 was testing EMD's new 645 engine and AR20 alternator; trailing it is EMD's test car (dynamometer) ET-909. *J. David Ingles*

This group included six ex-UP B units that the C&NW acquired from Amtrak (cheaply, no doubt) and rebuilt in 1973 with cabs and noses, giving them a distinctive—few say "attractive—appearance, like a cross between an E and a cowl unit. They were known as "Crandall Cab" engines after their designer, C&NW's then-superintendent of motive power, M.H. Crandall. They survived into the mid-1980s. New locomotives bumped C&NW Es and Fs from commuter service by 1993.

Milwaukee Road also operated E units in Chicago, with seven HEP-equipped E units

Canadian National F7 no. 9100 has been converted to a B unit, with control equipment removed, windshield and number boards blanked, and a larger fuel tank added (along with extra weight). It's at Sarcee Yard in Calgary, Alb., in June 1983. *Mike Chandler*

Among the last places to go to see matched sets of F units in operation was northern Minnesota, where Erie Mining still ran its F9s on iron ore trains. An A-B-B-B set carries taconite pellet loads toward the railroad's dock on Lake Superior in July 1988.
Steve Glischinski

Several former Gulf, Mobile & Ohio F3s earned new life in 1979 when they were rebuilt by Illinois Central's Paducah Shops, which termed them "FP10s." They served in commuter service for Massachusetts Bay Transportation Authority into the 1990s.
Trains magazine collection

on Nortran (North Suburban Mass Transit) service until 1978.

In the east, a couple dozen E units served several commuter routes out of New York City and Boston through the 1970s (some into the 1980s). Most were ex-Conrail, including former New York Central, Pennsylvania, and Erie Lackawanna locomotives. Penn Central had 28 E7s as of late 1971, and a few ex-PRR E7s ran on its New York & Long Branch commuter trains into the late 1970s.

F units on the decline

The oldest locomotives are usually the first to be retired, and this was certainly the case with FTs as railroads began retiring and trading them in beginning in the mid-1950s. The FTs in particular were a technological step behind later Fs. They weren't as powerful, didn't lend themselves to rebuilding, and they were becoming both maintenance and operational headaches. They had been used hard, with many racking up millions of miles in mainline service, and were simply worn out.

Thanks to effective marketing by EMD, an appealing trade-in program allowed railroads to turn in FTs and have them "rebuilt" into new road switchers. With these, the body was scrapped and many components were reconditioned, but not necessarily re-used in the new locomotives being ordered. This was basically a way to

Santa Fe still had about 400 F units in service when "bluebonnet" scheme F7 343 was photographed at Cleburne, Texas, in May 1972. Their numbers would drop rapidly during the decade, either to retirement or rebuilding. *J. David Ingles*

provide trade-in credit beyond scrap value toward new locomotives. This started during GP9 production, but grew more popular with EMD's introduction of the GP20 and SD24, which became the first of what became known as "second-generation" diesels—the diesels that replaced early diesels, as opposed to the first-generation diesels that replaced steam.

The first railroad to take advantage of this on a large scale was Boston & Maine, which in 1957 traded in its entire fleet of 48 FTs (built in 1943-1944) toward credit for 50 new GP9s. Other railroads followed suit; by the mid-1960s, operational FTs were hard to find. The last in service in the U.S. were Northern Pacific A-B set 5409D-C, which in 1970 were traded to EMD.

Many later-model Fs, especially late F3s through F9s, enjoyed longer lives. Unlike E units, which faced the loss of passenger traffic in the 1960s, railroads still had plenty of freight trains for F units to carry; however, they were usually demoted from their original mainline priority-freight assignments. By 1970, the locomotive newsmagazine *Extra 2200 South* estimated that about half of the nearly 7,600 F units built were still in service. Several railroads still operated large numbers of them into the 1970s: Santa Fe, owner of more Fs than any other railroad (nearly 900), still had 400 running as of 1972.

These numbers dropped dramatically in the next few years. The late 1960s had seen a surge of locomotive rebuilding that would last through the late 1970s. Railroads, along with outside contractors, found they could rebuild engines and completely recondition other components and get what amounted to a new locomotive at a significantly lower cost. However, most of these efforts focused on GP7s and GP9s rather than F units because of the F's design shortcomings with visibility and internal access.

Because Fs didn't have as much value on the rebuild or second-hand market as old GP7s or GP9s, a majority of railroads retired and scrapped or traded-in their F units on new power. By 1978, in a *Trains* magazine article surveying operational E and F units, author J. David Ingles noted that by that year only about 10 percent of Fs built—775—were still in operation. And that number was shrinking rapidly. Burlington Northern, Canadian National, and Conrail all still each had more than 100 in service, but they were retiring them quickly.

The recession of 1980 to 1982 hit railroads hard, with traffic and carloadings down. Orders for new locomotives dropped significantly, and with less demand for motive power, railroads stored and retired a lot of locomotives, namely older, less-powerful engines—such as F units—as well as those from minor manufacturers and other oddball locomotives.

By the early 1980s, few F units remained in operation; exceptions were largely passenger locomotives in commuter service and a few in service on short lines.

Last fleets

Canadian Pacific and Canadian National preferred GMD F and FP diesels in passenger service (along with Alco's FPA and FPB models). Many survived through the 1970s

The F units lasting longest in regular service were the former New Haven FL9s. Here Conrail no. 5040 and a sister in weathered Penn Central paint lead Train 948 at North White Plains in June 1978. The smoke is from celebratory torpedoes placed on the tracks to commemorate retiring engineer Harry Morton's final run. *J.W. Swanberg*

until the formation of VIA Rail Canada with the spinoff of CN's passenger operations in 1977 and the addition of CP equipment and operations in 1978. Much like Amtrak did with E units, VIA selected the newest locomotives from those available, with FP9s and F9Bs surviving the longest. While waiting for new locomotive orders to be approved, VIA had 15 FP9s rebuilt at CN's Pointe Ste. Charles shops from 1983 to 1985, with the original 567C engines receiving 645E power assemblies. Some of these rebuilds, designated FP9ARM, remained in service until 2001.

Another notable group was the 19 F units owned by Massachusetts Bay Transportation Authority. In 1979, MBTA contracted with Illinois Central's Paducah (Ky.) Shops (best known for its "Paducah Rebuild" Geeps) to rebuild 19 former Gulf, Mobile & Ohio F3s into what Paducah termed "FP10s." They retained their carbodies and had their 567B engines rebuilt. Most (15) received HEP (head-end-power) units, with four retaining steam generators.

Visually the main change was the addition of stainless-steel grilles over the upper side openings, the elimination of the side

Rock Island no. 630 would become the last E6 in service, pulling commuter trains in Chicago through the 1970s. It's shown here at Armourdale Yard in Kansas City in April 1963. *Frank Tatnall*

In the 1970s Santa Fe rebuilt more than 200 of its F units into what it termed CF7s. Nothing much remained to indicate their F unit heritage, however. The rebuilt locomotives were road switchers on new frames.
Charles M. Mizell, Jr.

portholes, the addition of five distinctive covers over the side air-intake openings (cut-down Far-Air grilles), a large winterization hatch, marker lights above each number board, and protective grilles over the windshields. These were retired by MBTA in the early 1990s; some went to Metro-North and operated a few more years, and others went to tourist lines.

Another group of Fs in commuter service were five former Baltimore & Ohio F7s rebuilt by Morrison-Knudsen for Maryland Department of Transportation in 1981. These retained their 567 engines, but were rebuilt with HEP units.

Two non-passenger groups of Fs were notable for their long lives, both in iron ore service. Erie Mining (later LTV Steel), a 73-mile, non-common carrier line in northern Minnesota, carried taconite pellets from an inland processing plant to a dock on Lake Superior. The railroad bought 11 F9s (5 A units, 6 Bs) new in 1956 and the fleet stayed relatively intact through the 1990s. The railroad became a favorite with railfans, as matched sets of F9s were a common sight until the plant and railroad operations ceased in 2001.

Another iron ore line known for its Fs—but isolated and difficult to get to for photography—was U.S. Steel's Atlantic City, Wyo., operation. The 77-mile railroad hauled ore from the company's mine and processing plant to a Union Pacific connection near Rock Springs. It had an all-F7 (ex-Bessemer & Lake Erie) fleet, and regularly operated Fs in matched A-B-B-B-B-A consists until the mine closed and operations ceased in 1983.

Another group that had a surprisingly long life was the New Haven's fleet of 60 dual-power (electric/diesel-electric) FL9s. The last F units built, they were successful in service, but never fully achieved their goals of replacing electric locomotives in passenger service. Their unique dual-service mode gave them long lives.

The locomotives passed from New Haven to Penn Central with the 1968 merger (bankrupt New Haven was added as a condition of the Pennsylvania/New York Central merger), but they suffered from various levels of neglect—as with

Burlington E5 no. 9911A, along with an articulated train set from the *Nebraska Zephyr*, was restored and maintained in operating condition by the Illinois Railway Museum. It's at Oshkosh, Wis., on an excursion outing in September 1993.
Jeff Wilson

One of the original FT demonstrator A units, along with another FTB, have been cosmetically restored to their original appearance. Shown here at an EMD open house, they normally reside at the National Museum of Transportation in St. Louis.
Trains magazine collection

other locomotives and infrastructure in the Northeast Corridor.

Most remained in service until the formation of Conrail in 1976, when a dozen FL9s went to Amtrak (half were operable; the other six were scavanged for parts; Amtrak had been leasing some FL9s from PC starting in 1974). Amtrak had the six rebuilt from 1978-80 by Morrison-Knudsen, including adding HEP. Amtrak extensively rebuilt them yet again in the early 1990s in its Beech Grove Shops, including replacing the original 567C engines with EMD 645E engines and upgrading the electrical and control equipment to Dash-2 standards. These survived in service into the 2000s.

Conrail's remaining FL9s continued in service until Metro-North took over its commuter operations in 1982; four of the locomotives were transferred to Connecticut Department of Transportation, which had them rebuilt by Chrome Crankshaft in 1985.

A former Soo Line F unit awaits the cutting torch at Pielet Brothers scrapyard in Chicago in 1980. It's the fate that awaited most E and F units when their service lives ended.
Paul Schneider

These were also repainted to original NH McGinnis colors.

Of Metro-North's fleet, seven had been rebuilt by General Electric in 1980. The agency in 1987 had 10 rebuilt by ABB-Traction using AC traction motors and equipment, essentially gutting the locomotives. Along with electrical gear, the 16-cylinder 567C engines were replaced with 12-cylinder EMD 710G engines. Of these, seven went to Metro-North (2040-46) and three to Long Island Rail Road (nos. 300-302). These were given the designation FL9AC.

More than 40 FL9s were still in service in 1992; the last of the Metro-North locomotives were retired in 2008.

CF7 rebuilds

Santa Fe had the largest fleet of F units—nearly 900—and in 1970 decided to rebuild many of its remaining F3s and F7s (but no FTs) by remanufacturing the engine and refurbishing (but re-using) the trucks, generator, and other major components. The railroad's Cleburne shops, which was also rebuilding older Geeps, eventually turned out 233 F unit rebuilds through early 1978. The Santa Fe called these rebuilt locomotives CF7s.

The resulting locomotives, however, looked nothing like the F units that entered the shops. To make the rebuilds useful for switching and secondary service, the Santa Fe turned them into road switchers, abandoning the streamlined carbody, building new underframes, and fabricating a new body and cab above the frame. The resulting locomotives looked much like the railroad's rebuilt Geeps, but with stubbier noses. The only nod to an F was that on early rebuilds, the cab retained the original curve of the F unit roof; this was later abandoned for an easier-to-fabricate angled cab roof.

The Santa Fe operated its CF7s into the mid-1980s before selling them off; they wound up on dozens of short lines and regional railroads, and many served for an additional 20 years.

Survivors

Although most Es and Fs were simply scrapped after retirement, we're lucky that many have been preserved and cosmetically or operationally restored. Notable among these are four early (slant-nose) Es, including Atlantic Coast Line 501 (an E3 rebuilt to an E6 before delivery) at the North Carolina Transportation Museum and Chicago, Burlington & Quincy E5 9911A, which carries trains with a restored, articulated *Nebraska Zephyr* train set at the Illinois Railway Museum.

Several F units and later Es have been preserved, including many in operating condition, and they can be found at museums, shortline operations, and tourist lines across the country. Notable among Fs are an FT A-B set at the National Museum of Transportation in St. Louis. The A unit is one of the original demonstrator FTs (which later went to Southern), and it (with another B) has been cosmetically restored in the original demonstrator scheme.

BIBLIOGRAPHY

BOOKS

Burlington's Zephyrs, by Karl Zimmermann. MBI Publishing Co., 2004.

The Complete Book of North American Railroading, by Kevin EuDaly et al. Voyageur Press, MBI Publishing, 2009.

The Diesel from D to L, by Vernon L. Smith. Kalmbach Publishing Co., 1979

Diesels West! by David P. Morgan. Kalmbach Publishing Co., 1963.

Doodlebug Country, by Edmund Keilty, 1982

E Units: Electro-Motive's Classic Streamliners, by Jeff Wilson. Kalmbach Publishing Co., 2002.

The Early Zephyrs, by Geoffrey H. Doughty. TLC Publishing, 2002.

Electro-Motive E Units and F Units, by Brian Solomon. Voyageur Press/MBI Publishing, 2011.

EMD F-Unit Locomotives, by Brian Solomon. Specialty Press, 2005.

F Units: The Diesels That Did It, by Jeff Wilson. Kalmbach Publishing Co., 2000.

Guide to North American Diesel Locomotives, by Jeff Wilson. Kalmbach Media, 2017.

The Historical Guide to North American Railroads, Third Edition. Kalmbach Publishing Co., 2014

Interurbans Without Wires, by Edmund Keilty, 1979.

Model Railroader Cyclopedia, Vol. 2: Diesel Locomotives, compiled by Bob Hayden. Kalmbach Publishing, 1980.

The Revolutionary Diesel: EMC's FT, by Diesel Era. Withers Publishing, 1994.

Rock Island Motive Power, by Lloyd E. Stagner. Pruett Publishing Co., 1980.

Union Pacific Railroad, by Brian Solomon. MBI Publishing, 2000.

PERIODICALS

"The 100-Class FTs," by Wally Abbey, *Warbonnet* (Santa Fe Railway Historical & Modeling Society), 3rd Quarter 1997, p. 7.

"All About Fs," by Dan Dover, *Extra 2200 South*, January 1970, p. 19.

"Amtrak Roster," by Dick Will, *Extra 2200 South*, November-December 1973, p. 13.

"Baldwin: The Bigger They Are, the Harder They Fall," by Greg McDonnell, *Diesel Victory, Classic Trains Special Edition No. 4,* 2006, p. 50.

"Better Trains follow Better Locomotives," by Greg Palumbo, *Classic Trains*, Summer 2012, p. 56.

"This Bulldog Gets No Respect" (FP7s), by J. David Ingles, *Classic Trains*, Spring 2015, p. 56.

"Concerning a Dipstick, Derby Day, Slack-Free Starts, 74 Degrees Below Zero, A Lonely E9, and May 18, 1942," by David P. Morgan, *Trains*, September 1972, p. 46.

"Covered Wagons ... The Circle Grows Smaller," by J. David Ingles, *Trains*, July 1978, p. 26.

"The Diesel that Did It," by David P. Morgan, *Trains*, February 1960, p. 18.

"E is for Efficient, Elegant, Elite ..." by Jim Sandrin, *Burlington Bulletin No. 10*, p. 4 (Burlington Route Historical Society).

"E Units: A through 9," by Preston Cook, *Trains*, June 2012, p. 20.

"E7 Roster," by Dan Dover and Dick Will, *Extra 2200 South*, May/June 1972, p. 25.

"E8/E9 Roster," by Dan Dover, *Extra 2200 South*, November/December 1973, p. 15.

"Early Days at LaGrange," by Milo M. Schalla, *Classic Trains*, Spring 2015, p. 48.

"Electro-Motive: From Upstart to Undisputed Champ," by Greg McDonnell, *Diesel Victory, Classic Trains Special Edition No. 4*, 2006, p. 20.

"Electro-Motive's FT Celebrates 50 Years," parts 1, 2, and 3, by Preston Cook, *Railfan & Railroad*, October 1989, p. 46; November 1989, p. 48; December 1989, p. 76.

"The Essence of the E7," by David P. Morgan, *Trains*, January 1979, p. 30.

"Exploring the Kansas City Southern," by J. David Ingles, *Classic Trains*, Summer 2012, p. 62.

"F Units: T through 9," by Preston Cook, *Classic Trains*, Spring 2015, p. 20.

"How the Diesel Changed Railroading," by Jerry A. Pinkepank, *Diesel Victory, Classic Trains Special Edition No. 4*, 2006, p. 8.,

"The Indestructible Locomotive" (E7s), by J.W. Hawthorne, *Trains*, January 1979, p. 44

"Inside an E Unit," by Preston Cook, *Classic Trains*, Summer 2012, p. 54.

"Inside an F Unit," by Preston Cook, *Classic Trains*, Spring 2015, p. 54.

"The Knickerbocker Super Chief," by Michael E. Eden, *Classic Trains*, Summer 2012, p. 46

"The LaGrange Influence," by David P. Morgan, *Trains*, September 1972, p. 30.

"LaGrange Locomotive Landmarks," *Trains*, September 1972, p. 38.

"Letter from FT 103," by Eric Hirsimaki, *Diesel Victory, Classic Trains Special Edition No. 4*, 2006, p. 102.

"Lima: Last In, First to Leave," by Greg McDonnell, *Diesel Victory, Classic Trains Special Edition No. 4*, 2006, p. 80.

"Marketing and Delivering the FT," by Preston Cook, *Classic Trains*, Spring 2015, p. 36.

"Martin Blomberg, Designer Extraordinaire," by Max Ephraim, Jr., *Trains*, October 1994, p. 46.

"Martin Blomberg, Streamliner Designer," by Carl R. Byron, *Classic Trains*, Summer 2012, p. 38.

"Mr. Brooks and the Beardmores," by Kevin J. Holland, *Diesel Victory, Classic Trains Special Edition No. 4*, 2006, p. 82.

"New England's Only FTs," by Jim Shaughnessy, *Classic Trains*, Spring 2015, p. 42.

"Playing With Fire: The Saga of the FL9," by J.W. Swanberg, *Classic Trains*, Spring 2015, p. 78.

"Re-Engineering the FT," by Preston Cook, *Classic Trains*, Spring 2015, p. 39.

"A Reputation for Reliability" (E7s), by W.A. Gardner, *Trains*, January 1979, p. 48.

"Shovelnoses," by Hol Wagner, *Burlington Bulletin, No. 13* (Burlington Route Historical Society).

"Those Early Es," by Louis A. Marre, *Extra 2200 South*, April 1968, p. 19.

"The Trouble With E Units, Part 1: The Winton-Engined Units," by Preston Cook, *Railfan & Railroad*, October 2008, p. 30.

"The Trouble With E Units, Part 2: The 567 Begins its Reign," by Preston Cook, *Railfan & Railroad*, November 2008, p. 44.

"The Trouble With E Units, Part 3: The E8 and E9," by Preston Cook, *Railfan & Railroad*, December 2008, p. 50.

"The Unsinkable FL9," by Scott A. Hartley, *Trains*, March 1993, p. 34.

MISC. SOURCES

Electro-Motive E and F unit operating manuals and specification books/pamphlets, various editions.

"Hearing Before the Subcommittee on Antitrust and Monopoly of the Committee on the Judiciary, United States Senate, 84th Congress, First Session," December 9, 1955, U.S. Government Printing Office, Washington, 1956.

"History and Development of the 567 Series General Motors Locomotive Engine," paper by E.W. Kettering, Chief Engineer, Electro-Motive Division of General Motors, November 29, 1951.

Locomotive Cyclopedia, various editions. Simmons-Boardman Publishing.

Locomotive Reference Data (periodical), General Motors Electro-Motive Division, 1950 and 1957 editions